PART I

I Will Think of Everything You, Think Only of Loving Me

The life-changing
Littlest Way of Love
as revealed to
Venerable Sister Consolata Betrone
and experienced by
A Sister of Children of Mary

PART II

The Littlest Way of Love

Abridged message
from the Heart of Jesus to
Venerable Sister Consolata Betrone

By
Fr. Lorenzo Sales, IMC

In accord with the *Code of Canon Law*, I hereby grant the *Imprimatur* ("Permission to Publish") regarding the manuscript entitled *The Ceaseless Act of Love.*

Imprimatur: ☩ Most Reverend Joseph R. Binzer
Auxiliary Bishop
Vicar General
Archdiocese of Cincinnati
April 5, 2017

The *Imprimatur* ("Permission to Publish") is a declaration that a book or pamphlet is considered free of doctrinal or moral error. It is not implied that those who have granted the *Imprimatur* agree with the contents, opinions or statements expressed.

I Will Think of Everything. You, Think Only of Loving Me
The Ceaseless Act of Love

ISBN 978-1523273485

love for Love Publishing

5440 Moeller Ave
Cincinnati, OH 45212
www.childrenofmary.net

Dedicated to the Heart of Jesus
To the glory of God, the Father

CHILDREN of *Mary*

5440 Moeller Ave.
Cincinnati, OH 45212

Very Dear Friends of Children of Mary,

The feedback we are getting from our book is incredible. Thousands of copies have been sent out and orders keep pouring in – most of them for multiple copies, from 4-50! The most common comment we receive is, "this book is changing my life."

Evidently, this book, what Jesus said to Venerable Sr. Consolata, is helping a lot of people. We are filled with joy that ceaseless acts of love are going up to the throne of God and gladdening His Heart and, at the same time, bringing peace, strength and joy to His people. Living this message *will* change your life *and* help the world, for, as St. John of the Cross said, "the smallest act of pure love is worth more to the Church than all works put together!"

The world is growing ever darker and colder. But, you don't have to feel helpless! Live the message and love will save the world. We pray you will share the book with as many others as possible. We are confident that God will reward you greatly.

To order more books visit: www.childrenofmary.net
email: childrenofmarysisters@gmail.com
OR call: (513) 713-0432

The suggested donation is $12 per book but if this amount would be a burden to you – please let us know!

PART I

I Will Think of Everything You, Think Only of Loving Me

By
A Sister of
Children of Mary

"The more that you love Me,
the happier that you will be.
And every act of love will save a soul."
(Jesus to Venerable Sister Consolata Betrone)

Table of Contents

1

"I will do all the thinking.
You, think only of loving Me."

These few words are changing my life

A few months ago I was introduced to the messages Jesus entrusted to Servant of God Sister Consolata Betrone, a Capuchin nun who was born in 1903 and died in 1946. I want to share it with as many people as possible. I believe it is a message for our time, a time when the storm clouds are gathering in our country--indeed in our world--that could likely be the test of tests for many of us. Those who are striving to live this message will, I believe, have a strength and wisdom from on high that will help them not only cope, but maintain peace of soul in the midst of suffering, something the saints have shown us is possible with the grace of God.

This is how I found out about it. One afternoon I received a call from one of my Sisters who was at the Newark Motherhouse on retreat. She had been given a booklet to use during her retreat called "The Littlest Way," a booklet that had been sent to us by a young lady preparing to enter a cloistered monastery in Indiana, *The Poor Sisters of St. Clare.* I had not read the booklet, but trusted it was something very good, since it is a favorite devotion of a woman we respect very much, the Mother Superior of the Poor Sisters. Sister called me and said, "Do you know what Our Lord said to Sr. Consolata? He said that He will think of everything. He wants us to think only of loving Him! And then He said, "I am asking a continuous act of love from you, from the moment you rise in the morning until you go to bed at night: 'Jesus, Mary, I love You. Save souls.'" As she spoke those words, my heart was burning; and with great desire, I replied, "That is what I want! I want my life to be a continuous act of love!"

Then she went on to tell a little more of what Jesus had said to Sr. Consolata:

> "Love Me continually. It doesn't matter if your heart is made of stone or ice!"

> "The more you love Me, the happier you will be."

> "Each act of love saves a soul from eternal damnation."

When I got off the phone I said to the Lord, "I don't know how this could work--You do all the thinking and I think only of loving You. I have a very important decision to make this evening." The decision I had to make was important: I had been praying and discerning about it for two months. Then it was time for my Holy Hour with the Lord. I knew I had two choices: I could go to the Holy Hour and do what I would normally have done--spend the whole time thinking about this situation and praying for guidance, or I could go in and practice the continuing acts of love. So I said to the Lord, "I don't understand how this can work, but I am going to try it." I spent the hour in prayer, doing my best to make continuous acts of love. I was amazed that I did not once think about the decision that had been weighing on me. After the Holy Hour, we chanted the Divine Office, and again God gave me the grace not to ponder the decision. Then the time came to go to the meeting. As I was walking down the hall I felt much peace, even though I didn't have a clue what I was going to say. Then I heard in my heart the Lord telling me a question to ask at the meeting. So I went in and did just that. After about an hour and a half of listening to the answer to that question, I had no doubt at all what my decision was.

I was quite impressed. I had not wasted my Holy Hour nor been distracted during Divine Office trying to discern God's will--I simply did my best to think of nothing but loving Jesus. And He did what He said He would do: He thought of everything; and, because I had made acts of love, He guided me in what to say and do!

Another time, two of us were travelling and were about an hour away from our destination when the phone rang. It was one of my Sisters; the news was not good. She told me about a difficult situation we would be facing when we arrived. After we talked I grabbed my rosary and began praying aloud. On each Our Father bead I said the words Jesus had said to Sr. Consolata, "I will do all the thinking. You, think only of loving Me." On each Hail Mary bead I made an act of love, "Jesus, Mary, I love You. Save souls." In the past I would have spent that hour worrying or thinking about the situation, or asking myself questions to which I had no answer, which made this type of thinking useless, a waste of time. I continued praying this Chaplet of the Ceaseless Act of Love aloud continuously until we arrived. I was filled with peace as we dealt with the situation, and--thanks be to God--all ended well. This experience was a gift from God for which I am very grateful. He gave me the grace to remain calm and to peacefully let His plan unfold and deal with each moment as He led. I hope and pray that He will continue to give me such graces in the future, for I know that how I reacted that day was not how I would have normally acted. Oh, I would not have been a nervous wreck and gotten all excited, but neither would I have had the interior peace and calm that I had that day.

Just one more story. One afternoon a woman came to me wrestling with a problem. I fell into my usual mode and tried to solve the problem, giving advice and suggesting solutions, although it was a problem I could not solve. After we talked, I went into the chapel and said to the Lord, "I just blew it. I was trying to do all the thinking and not thinking only of loving You." Then I heard in my heart, "Stay out of it. It is between Me and her." I immediately felt relief. I didn't have to solve anything--God would take care of it! Then I was able to pray. Not long after that, I read a quote from St. John of the Cross telling us, in effect, not to be overly upset with the problems of others, because each of us must work out his own salvation. Lord, will I ever be able to make my life a ceaseless act of love? There is much to learn in order to control our thoughts and our words. But thank God, He is patient and wants to teach us, if only we persevere in the struggle.

Soon I began to share these experiences with others. Almost everyone I shared with immediately began practicing this Littlest Way, and they shared with me what a help it was to them. Then one of our lay missionaries came to our Motherhouse for retreat and had a powerful experience one night during adoration. I share it with you because it is quite profound. As you ponder it, I pray it will enrich your prayer as it has mine. Here is her story.

****
****

Shortly after Sister had shared with me The Littlest Way of Love, I went on a retreat at the Children of Mary Motherhouse in Newark, Ohio. During a Holy Hour on that retreat, I was kneeling in front of our Lord in the Most Blessed Sacrament holding a relic of the true Cross. As I knelt there, I began to hear a loud roar of blasphemies and mockeries being hurled from the crowd to Jesus on the Cross. It was so painful to witness these displays of arrogance and to hear all this hatred being spewed onto Jesus as He hung on the Cross in such agony, suffering and dying for their sins and mine.

People of all generations were shouting out blasphemies by words and by their sinful actions of the past, present, and future. It was an accumulation of what was present to Jesus Christ on Calvary, because He took on ALL sin of ALL time. As

Padre Pio wrote in his booklet, The Agony of Jesus:

"All our sins with their entire ugliness parade before Him in every detail. He sees all the meanness and the malice of creatures in committing them. He knows to what extent these sins offend and outrage the Majesty of God. He see all the infamies, immodesties, blasphemies which proceed from the lips of creatures accompanied by the malice of their hearts, of those hearts and those lips which were created to bring forth hymns of praise and benediction to the Creator. . . . . He must clothe Himself with this entire unclean mass of human corruption and present Himself before the sanctity of His Father, to expiate everything with individual pains, to render Him all that glory of which they have robbed Him; to cleanse that human cesspool in which man wallows with contemptible indifference."

I remember very clearly that there was a real strong sense of not just the noise of the blasphemies being shouted directly at Jesus, but also the deafening silence of so many people just following the crowd, indifferent, self-absorbed, distracted. So many people in all generations not focused on the meaning and the calling of Jesus' suffering and death on the Cross, not being sorry for their sins that put Him there, and not being truly grateful and awed by the magnitude of His love for us in this great act of redemption. I sensed these blasphemies of indifference contributing IMMENSELY to His suffering of being alone and abandoned and then on top of that to know that many of these people might never respond to the grace of redemption He is offering to them. This indifference was excruciating to our Savior.

My heart ached for Him as I felt His deep aloneness, rejected and tortured by His own creatures, by those whom He created out of love and for love. He was suffering so greatly to save the very creatures who offend Him. I tried to catch the eyes of Jesus as He looked across the crowd looking for love. It was as if He was crying out with His eyes from the very depths of His being, "Does anyone care? Is anyone grateful? Will you respond to the graces I obtain for you by My suffering and dying in your place?" I began to call His name louder and louder, "Jesus! Jesus! Jesus! I care! I am so sorry for all the pain I've caused you by my sins! Thank you for dying for me! Please never let me be separated from you again!"

Then I saw Mary, near the foot of the cross, in such pain as she witnessed the cruelty of all these horrible blasphemies, including the contemptible blasphemies of indifference, coming from the very people her Son was suffering and dying for, those whom He loved so much. I knew that Mary, too, in her great motherly love for us, longed for the salvation of all those people, just as her Son did. She was willing, no matter how incredibly painful it was, to give the fruit of her life --Jesus-- so that others might live. And that's when I remembered to say, "Jesus, Mary, I love You! Save souls!" As I kept repeating that, I noticed that the Children of Mary Sisters and others had joined me in standing near Mary. They also were saying,

"Jesus, Mary, I love You! Save souls!"

As we continued to focus our undivided love and attention on Jesus and Mary, the crowd of people gathering to cry out their love just kept growing and growing. Soon that crowd was down the hill and spreading in the distance as far as I could see. There were throngs of people; we were all raising our voices in unison, "Jesus, Mary, I love You! Save souls!" giving them support and cheering them on.

Our voices were drowning out the blasphemies and insults, so that our Lord and Savior, Jesus Christ, and His Mother could hear that their great love and sacrifices really were being noticed and appreciated--that they truly are loved in return, love for Love. This growing crowd of people recognized that Jesus, Who had no sin, was taking our place to give us a chance for eternal life with Him in heaven. What a gift!! We are and will be eternally grateful for that gift.

The symphony of our love will drown out the blasphemies and hatred and, the more subtle but very real pain, inflicted on Jesus and Mary by indifference. Hopefully, more and more people will be drawn to repent and join us in the chorus of love for Love, "Jesus, Mary, I love You! Save souls!"

A Lay Missionary with the Children of Mary

****
****

I'm just beginning to learn this new way of thinking and of being. The more I live it, as imperfectly as it is at this stage, the more profound and life changing I realize it can be. I beg the grace to persevere in doing my best to practice it until my dying breath, for even in the short time I have done it, many blessings have resulted.

It is quite demanding, what Jesus tells us to do, not to think of anything but loving Him. In fact, it is humanly impossible. Jesus knows that, and that it will be a matter of strongly willing it and doing our best to do it. It is part of the plan that we grow in grace as we struggle to rid our minds of useless thoughts and our lips of unnecessary words. Our Lord doesn't want us to get discouraged when we fail frequently. It is like a child learning to walk and talk. It is all new, and we learn as we stumble and keep getting up to try again.

So, too, is it with the continuous act of love. But the journey in growing in this act of love is exciting. Yet, they tell me for those who persevere for a long period of time, it can become arduous. But it is worth the effort. I believe that for those who do take this seriously, it will be like a sharing in the life of Mother Mary, Whose entire life was surely one continuous, profound, perfect act of love. Of course, no one can reach the level of sanctity Our Lady reached; She is holier than all the angels and saints put together! But She loves us and will intercede for us with Her powerful prayers so that we, too, can make our lives a ceaseless act of love.

2

Jesus, Mary, I love You. Save souls.

Why is Mary in the Act of Love?

Sr. Consolata said that the act of love that Jesus prefers is: "Jesus, Mary, I love You. Save souls." As I began making this act of love, I wondered why He wanted Mary to be included in it. After our lay missionary reported the experience she had had in prayer, it made sense. She said that Jesus was hearing nothing but blasphemies, and as He hung there in agony, He looked around, and: "It was as if He was crying out with His eyes from the very depths of His being, 'Does anyone care? Is anyone grateful? Will you respond to the graces I obtain for you by My suffering and dying in your place?' Then I saw Mary, near the foot of the cross, in such pain as she witnessed the cruelty of all these horrible blasphemies, including the contemptible blasphemies of indifference, coming from the very people her Son was suffering and dying for, those whom He loved so much. I knew that Mary too, in her great motherly love for us, longed for the salvation of all those people just as Her Son did. She was willing, no matter how incredibly painful it was, to give the fruit of her life, Jesus, so that others might live."

So that must be why Jesus' favorite act of love includes Mary: "Jesus, Mary, I love You. Save souls." Mary suffered an interior martyrdom at the foot of the Cross--suffering more than we could ever imagine. She is Co-Redemptrix.

That term, Co-Redemptrix, is often misunderstood among our Protestant brothers and sisters, and even among some Catholics, who think we are equating Mary and Jesus. We are not. Mary is a human person; Jesus is a Divine Person. Only God could redeem us because sin is an offense against God. To be a co-redeemer is for those who are in union with Christ; that is, those who are in the state of grace and who unite their sufferings with Christ's as an offering to the Father to save souls.

We are all called to be co-redeemers. St. Paul said, "I make up in my own body what is lacking in the sufferings of Christ for the sake of His Body, that is, the Church." (Col. 1:24) I quoted that Scripture in a Catholic prayer group once, and a woman there looked at me shocked and said, "Heresy!" I replied, "I didn't say it; St. Paul did." And I showed her the Scripture. How could anything be lacking in the sufferings of Christ? Fr. Hardon explains that nothing could be lacking in the sufferings of Christ unless He willed it to be so. And why would He will it so? He willed it so that we, His brothers and sisters, could share in the work of redemption and, thereby, merit to share in His glory. Jesus said to St. Faustina, "I thirst. I thirst for the salvation of souls. Help Me, My daughter, to save souls. Join your sufferings to My Passion and offer them to the heavenly Father for sinners."

12

St. Faustina knew that her sanctity was essential to be useful for the Church, so she desired to be a saint and strove for it, so that she could save many, many souls. Jesus said to her, "I am Thrice Holy, and I detest the smallest sin. I cannot love a soul which is stained with sin; but when it repents, there is no limit to My generosity toward it. My mercy embraces and justifies it. With My mercy, I pursue sinners along all their paths, and My Heart rejoices when they return to Me. I forget the bitterness with which they fed My Heart and rejoice at their return. Tell sinners that no one shall escape My Hand: if they run away from My Merciful Heart, they will fall into My Just Hands. Tell sinners that I am always waiting for them, that I listen intently to the beating of their heart... when will it beat for Me? Write, that I am speaking to them through their remorse of conscience, through their failures and sufferings, through thunderstorms, through the voice of the Church. And if they bring all My graces to naught, I begin to be angry with them, leaving them alone and giving them what they want.... The loss of each soul plunges Me into mortal sadness. You always console Me when you pray for sinners. The prayer most pleasing to Me is prayer for the conversion of sinners. Know, My daughter, that this prayer is always heard and answered." He also asked her to pray for the dying. "Pray as much as you can for the dying. By your entreaties, obtain for them trust in My mercy, because they have most need of trust, and have it the least. Be assured that the grace of eternal salvation for certain souls in their final moment depends on your prayer." Finally, "Hold firmly to this always. Be constantly on the watch, for many souls will turn back from the gates of hell and worship My mercy. But fear nothing, as I am with you. Know that of yourself you can do nothing."

To share in the work of redemption we must be in the state of grace, which means to be in union with God. One could give His life for another, or save a million lives; but, if he were not in the state of grace, those acts, or any good works, would not merit him entrance into Heaven. Jesus said that without Him we can do nothing. But united with Christ in grace-- living in His light and His love, Jesus' followers can do great good! Jesus told Bl. Dina Belanger that one person can make up for what is lacking in the lives of others by winning precious efficacious graces for their salvation. The deeper our union with God, the more powerful our prayers; deeper union comes with deeper love.

Mary was Co-Redemptrix par excellence, because She was without sin. She was His Mother and loved Him more than anyone ever has or ever will. She stood at the foot of the Cross and suffered--willingly cooperating with the Father's plan for the salvation of souls. When we willingly accept the crosses God allows to come into our lives, we, too, cooperate in the redemption of souls. A cross embraced is a gift—the value of which we will be able to understand only in Heaven. I read once that if angels could envy us, they would envy us for two things: that we can receive Jesus in Holy Communion, and that we can suffer. Jesus said to St. Faustina, "You will save more souls through prayer and suffering than will a missionary through

14

his teachings and sermons alone."

From the Cross Jesus gave us a great gift: He gave us His Mother to be our Mother! We are part of a Heavenly Family!   God is our Father, Jesus is our Brother, and Mary is our Mother. And She wants each of us to grow in holiness; because the more acts of love we make and the holier we become, the more we gladden the Heart of God, Whom She watched shed His last drop of Blood for love of us. She wants that Precious Blood to cleanse and unite as many souls as possible to Him, quenching His thirst to be loved. Pray to Her, and She will pray for you to Her Son, Who sits at the right hand of the Father interceding for us.

Efficacious - Effective

3

You must have such mastery over your thoughts and your words that the devil can't bother you in any way, and this mastery is a gift that the act of love gives you as a favor.

Mastery over Self

Since beginning to make acts of love, I have been given the grace to be more aware than ever before of my useless thoughts and my unnecessary words. It is a blessing in my life, and I want to share it with everyone who is interested. It's not that my prayer life before was slack. We pray about six hours every day, much of that in the sacred Presence of our Eucharistic Lord. I love Our Lord very much, and have a great desire for everyone to love Him. But living in community the past several years, I have faced many new situations and had to make many decisions every day. Many times I took these matters to Jesus to ask His help, or during the silence many thoughts would come to me concerning various matters with which I was dealing. But I am not doing that anymore; at least I am trying my best not to do it anymore! Now I keep reminding myself to let Him do all the thinking and that my part is to love Him. It has made a great difference; my prayer life has deepened, as well as my peace of soul, my love for God and for my Sisters and everyone. I read the book written by Fr.

Lorenzo Sales, IMC about Sr. Consolata and the messages entitled "Jesus Appeals to the World" which received the Imprimatur in 1955.

Jesus' message contains instructions to help practice the continuous act of love, such as, think of no one--good or bad--think only of loving Me. This is a great tool to cut down on rash judgments and critical thoughts, and even good thoughts that are okay; but, compared to an act of love, well, there is no comparison. Jesus told Sr. Consolata that **one act of love can save a soul from hell.**

He told her many more things that can have a profound effect on helping us love Him more.

> *"If the soul can keep calm, then she will remain master of herself; but if she is perturbed, then it is easy for her to fall."*

> *"Never let yourself be perturbed, never, never! For when you become perturbed, the devil is content, then his victory will be assured."*

Imagine how many people this could help! And, if practiced, how many friendships, marriages and even lives could be saved! Knowing that we open the door of our hearts to satan when we get perturbed is a great incentive to try to control our emotions and not get upset. To know this truth helps a lot, but it may not stop us from feeling perturbed at times. One day something happened that perturbed me. I asked the Lord what to do with this feeling, how to get rid of it. No answer. But He used one of the littlest ones in our community to help me.

On one of our days of reflection, this quote about not getting perturbed was given to each of the Sisters, along with the instruction to ponder the following question: "But what does one do when she finds herself getting perturbed?" We spent the day in prayer; and, at the end of the day, we got together to share our thoughts. One of the young Sisters shared that she thought it would be good to go to the foot of the Cross with Mary and look with love at Jesus suffering. Of course, the answer is to make acts of love! Jesus told Sr. Consolata: *"As long as you love, the devil can't cause a bad thought to enter into you because all of our faculties are absorbed by love; but if you were to stop loving, that would be when he could do so. That's why you must always love."*

4

*I am asking a continuous act of love from you
from the moment you rise in the morning
until you go to bed at night.*

Reasons to Persevere

It was a few months ago that I began trying to implement the continuous act of love. Until then, I never knew I had so many thoughts come into my mind almost constantly, and how hard it is to master my thoughts. Except for the times when the Lord gives me the grace to enter deep into prayer, I am finding that I can only make acts of love for very short periods of time. Jesus told Sr. Consolata that it is the devil who keeps us from making the acts of love continuous, but Jesus allows it because our struggle helps us grow in grace.

Knowing all the great benefits that come from acts of love, is it any wonder that the devil will do all he can to keep us from making them? But, "greater is He that is in you, than he that is in the world." (1 John 4:6,16) Jesus will help as we surrender everything to Him and do our best to live a life of ceaseless acts of love. We must forget about ourselves and not get discouraged about our inability to achieve this progeny of holiness as quickly as we would like. *Offspring*

In times when we find ourselves failing repeatedly, it could help us not to get discouraged if we remind ourselves that, even if I made one act of love, there was great benefit gained. And here are some of the things Our Lord said about the act of love that will help:

- Each act of love is one soul
- Each act of love increases my love for Jesus and Jesus' love for me
- Each act of love is worth infinitely more than all of the treasures on earth
- Each act of love helps me to put a maximum value on every instant of the day

We will grow ever deeper in union with God if we continue our act of love even when we don't feel any emotion of love. Jesus said to Sr. Consolata, ***"Love Me continually. It doesn't matter if your heart is made of stone or ice!"*** It is not easy to love when we don't feel like loving, but it is an error to believe that love involves sense emotion or feeling. In fact, when we choose to love when we don't feel like doing so, we prove that we do in fact love. For when we make acts of love and perform acts of charity when we feel like doing them, there is the great possibility of an admixture of self-love, doing a thing because it pleases us to do so. But when we make an act of love--in word or deed--when we don't feel like it, it is for God alone that we act, a pure act of love.

The love of God lies in the grace-aided will; it presupposes the intellect insofar as the will needs its co-operation to love, for the will is a blind faculty; but in practice one need only attend to the will. <u>A very high degree of love of God is quite compatible with an absence of any feeling or emotion, and even with the presence of a feeling of distaste for the service of God.</u> We have only to remember our Lord's Prayer in the Agony at Gethsemani to realize that. In fact, if one is going to achieve the heights of the spiritual life, it is necessary to pass through a stage where one's apparent spiritual activity is reduced to a dry act of willingness to conform one's self to God's Will, in the darkness of a sheer decision to believe in God without light of any sort. This does not mean that the emotions have not their part to play in the spiritual life. On the contrary, they can be a most effective aid to the real agent, which is the will working by faith. (*The Tremendous Lover, M. Eugene Boylan*)

There is much more to learn that can transform your life when you read Part II of this book, such as: virginity of spirit, virginity of the tongue, virginity of heart. These are things that bear the fruit of interior peace and joy that comes with deepening our union with God.

5

I will do all the thinking.
You, think only of loving Me.

Should I Spread It?
Can I Live It?

Yes, these words, "I will do all the thinking. You, think only of loving Me" pierced my heart, and I longed to live my life as a ceaseless act of love. But did the Lord want our Community to promote the messages from Sr. Consolata? Or was this a temptation to distract us from our charism, which is to spread love for Our Lord, specifically love for Him in the Most Blessed Sacrament. The terrible indifference towards Jesus in this august Sacrament causes Him tremendous suffering. In fact, He told St. Margaret Mary that it causes Him more suffering than anything else He endured during His Passion.

Could this be what I call "a temptation to do good"? By that I mean, it is not likely that those who are striving for holiness will commit grievous sins, so the devil will resort to tempting them to do good things, but a good other than the good God has destined for them to do. Could this be such a temptation? In my heart it seemed quite the contrary. Rather, it seemed like a means to *more fully* live our charism; a way to continue our adoration of Jesus Eucharistic outside of the chapel.

Then I read these words of Sr. Consolata: *"... I understand that in practice, an act of love gives Jesus to the soul, or increases its grace; it's like a Communion."*

At first those words disturbed me. Reading this, would some people think they could get the same grace at home by making acts of love, and then not bother to go to Mass? What a tragedy that would be! Nothing on earth can compare with the graces of attending Holy Mass. Jesus is God, and with God there is no time; going to Mass is like getting in a time machine and pushing a button that says: CALVARY; and then mystically, miraculously, we are at the foot of the Cross, which is a timeless event-- the one permanent act of salvation. When Jesus and the Jews went to the temple to worship, they offered a sacrifice to God, the sacrifice of a spotless lamb whose life was sacrificed to atone for their sins. Since Calvary, in the unbloody Sacrifice of the Mass, the People of God have as their sacrifice the spotless Lamb of God, Jesus, God Incarnate. The Holy Sacrifice of the Mass is the same sacrifice that Jesus offered on Calvary. As we devoutly attend the Spotless Victim's offering of Himself to our Father, we offer our lives along with Him to the Father. We become part of the offering and, consequently, part of the mission to save souls!

But back to my dilemma, we would never want to promote anything that would deter anyone from attending this most sacred act of worship possible on earth, the Holy Mass! Then I read the words of St. Thomas Aquinas, called the Angelic Doctor, the most prominent and respected theologian the

Church has ever known. St. Thomas tells us that a "complete spiritual Communion can even take place **when we are unable** to receive sacramentally, because the effect of a sacrament can be secured if it is received by desire." So it is true, this practice of a ceaseless act of love can make it possible to extend our deep union with God outside the time of adoring Him and receiving Him in Holy Communion. This is accomplished by our desire-- our deep love for Jesus and the desire to receive Him in Holy Communion.

Another reaction I had when I first heard that Jesus had said, *"I will do all the thinking. You, think only of loving Me."* was that it was very radical! I wanted to let Jesus do all the thinking and me think only of loving Him, but was it really possible? I decided to do some research to see if any other Saints had said anything similar. I discovered that they had. I reread things I had read over the years and found some similarities. When I had read them in the past, they did not have the same impact as when I read Jesus' words to Sr. Consolata. Perhaps it was because, like Sacred Scripture, you can read the same passage many times and then, all of a sudden, you read it and the Holy Spirit enables you to have a new understanding. Or perhaps it was because the wording and presentation from other Saints was somehow less dramatic and lessened the impact.

Jesus to Sr. Consolata:

> *Forget everything and everybody, and think only of loving Me more! Concentrate your every thought, every heartbeat, every silence upon this one thing: to love! Do not think of anything,*

anything, anything else but to love Me and to suffer with all possible love; that is sufficient.

St. Faustina - November 27, 1936

And God has given me to understand that there is but one thing that is of infinite value in His eyes, **and that is love of God; love, love and once again, love; and <u>nothing can compare with a single act of pure love of God</u>.**

Jesus told Sr. Consolata not to think of others, but to always think of loving Him. St. John of the Cross offers similar advice:

> You should consequently strive to be incessant in prayer, and in the midst of your corporal practices do not abandon it. Whether you eat, or drink, or speak, or converse with lay people, or do anything else, you should always do so with the desire for God and with your heart fixed on Him. **This is very necessary for inner solitude, which demands that the soul dismiss any thought that is not directed to God.**
>
> Do not think about others, neither good things nor bad. Even were you to live among devils, you should not turn the head of your thoughts to their affairs, but forget these things entirely and strive to keep your soul occupied purely and entirely in God.

This quote reminds me in a special way of St. Maximilian Kolbe, who, when at Auschwitz, living in the midst of horrific evil, loved everyone, even the guards. I once read a story that, when St. Maximilian was on the work line in Auschwitz, a guard started beating him. A fellow prisoner came to defend him and began hitting the guard. St. Maximilian said to him, "Please, son, don't hit your brother!" St. Maximilian never wrote about the continuous act of love, but he surely lived it. I highly recommend the book, <u>A Man for Others</u>, if you want to see what a life of continuous acts of love looks like.

6

Jesus said to Sr. Consolata, "Promise Me you will not interest yourself in Sister X either directly or indirectly. No matter whether she observes the rule or not, whether she follows the community life in all simplicity or takes extraordinary paths with subterfuges, never mind! Promise Me that you will not speak or think of it...

Never Mind What Others Do

In our own lives, for most of us--at present at least--our distress will come in less dramatic circumstances than those St. Maximilian Kolbe faced. Ours will more likely be small things, like that rude woman talking in church while I'm trying to pray! Or more serious matters but yet still not worthy of causing us to cease making acts of love— things like allowing ourselves to be distracted in prayer by the things we see: immodest dress, rude behavior, irreverence toward our Eucharistic Lord, etc. The Lord is telling us not to think of anything or anyone but Him, and that means not even those who are doing wrong. He doesn't want us to watch others and get upset with their inappropriate behavior, but to keep our calm and love Him. Our distress doesn't help us or anyone. In fact, it hurts us and even them, in the sense that, if we were making acts of love, we would all be receiving grace. Like St. Maximilian Kolbe in the concentration camp--loving everyone, even the guards who were committing cruelties--we can thus bring light and love where there is need of these beautiful reflections of God.

St. John of the Cross tells us, "Distress and worry ordinarily makes things worse and even does harm to the soul itself. The endurance of all with equanimity not only reaps many blessings, but also helps the soul to employ the proper remedy." And these words of St. Francis of Assisi: "By the anxieties and worries of this life, satan tries to dull man's heart and make a dwelling for himself there."

Jesus to St. Faustina: "It should be no concern to you how anyone else acts; you are to be My living reflection, through love and mercy. " She answered, "Lord, but they often take advantage of my goodness." "That makes no difference, My daughter. That is no concern of yours. As for you, be always merciful toward other people, and especially toward sinners."

Abandonment to Divine Providence helps us keep our tranquility even in the midst of storms. Accepting everything, even those things that are painful, as a gift from our loving Father is a key to being able to remain calm under all circumstances. And not only acceptance of all that He allows to happen to us, but also a prompt and generous performance of all that the Divine Will clearly asks of us. Love is the conformity of our will to God's will. If we look at the lives of the martyrs, we will see examples of this. As St. John de Brebeuf, a Jesuit missionary to the Hurons in Quebec, was being tortured, he continued to exhort those who were torturing him to accept Jesus as their Savior. Even as they sliced off the skin from his arms and legs, cooked it and ate it in front of him, and as they poured boiling hot water over his head three times as a mockery of baptism, he continued his dialogue of love to his people, for whom he willingly offered his life to God so as to gain graces for their conversion.

7

*Remember that a loving glance and a sweet smile
have a greater influence on a soul than the loveliest
sermon. Isn't it true that feeling yourself loved and
understood in a brotherly, holy manner can make the
Way of Perfection seem a lighter one to travel?
I keep pain for Myself, and I give smiles to souls;
you do the same.*

*Don't omit a single act of love for Me, see Me in
everyone and say a resolute "yes" to all,
with firm confidence that My help will never fail you.
And smile. Always smile.
I Myself will be smiling through you.*

Say "Yes" to All
with a Smile

Jesus tells us to always take notice of when others
need help, and to always say "yes" with a sweet
smile. And He said to do this not for the individual,
but for love of Him alone.

St. Claude La Colombiere made this astonishing
statement about charity. Read and ponder.

> "You love all your enemies, and you love them
> very tenderly, with the exception of only one;
> and you willingly forgive that one all the evil that
> he has done to you, with the exception of one

sole insult; and still you do not intend to take other revenge for it, if only that you would make for him a little less good and fewer signs of esteem than before. If you are in this disposition, Christian auditors, you have no Christian charity, no love for your neighbor. The authentic virtues are limited neither to certain times, nor to certain actions, nor to certain particular subjects. The one who possesses them is disposed to practice them in all things, in all encounters, with regard to all kinds of people, and in all ways."

If you abide in Me, and My words abide in you, you shall ask what you will, and it shall be done unto you. Herein is My Father glorified, that you bear much fruit; so shall you be My disciples. As the Father hath loved Me, so have I loved you: continue in My love. If you keep My commandments, you shall abide in My love; even as I have kept My Father's commandments, and abide in His love. These things have I spoken unto you, that My joy might remain in you, and that your joy might be full. (John 15: 7-11)

We may wonder at times at Jesus' words, "These things have I spoken unto you, that My joy might remain in you, and that your joy might be full." Perhaps we think, why don't I experience this joy? After reading what St. Claude La Colombiere said, we can understand; it is our lack of virtue. Jesus said, right before expressing His hope that His joy might be ours and that our joy might be full, that we are to keep His commandments *as He has kept His Father's commandments!* So could it be that our joy is commensurate with how perfectly we keep the commandments? Want joy? Let your heart ache to do whatever it takes to achieve this great union with Jesus! To abide in Him as He is in the Father! Let your heart burn with a great desire for deeper union with God. Let your prayer be: "What do You wish of me, Lord, that I may be one in You? With Your grace, I will do whatever it takes. Just tell me, Lord. Do you want me to give up the computer? My relationship with 'so and so'? Television? Sports? Show me everything and anything that keeps me from achieving deep union with You, and I will rid my life of it. Speak, Lord, I am listening."

8

...say a resolute "yes" to all

<u>Always</u> Say "Yes"??

Jesus asks for a ceaseless act of love of always saying "yes" to all. But did He really mean that we always say "yes" to everyone all the time? The answer is to say "yes" unless charity or duty require otherwise. Our Lord would never want us to neglect either of these two obligations. Our sanctity comes with doing what our state in life requires. A wife and mother would not become holy by spending several hours each day in prayer if that would result in neglecting her family duties.

The primary duty of husbands and wives is to help one another get to heaven and to be open to all the children God wants to give them. As parents, their primary duty is to provide for the physical, spiritual and emotional needs of the children. It is their solemn duty to pass on the Faith to them. Sometimes, this will mean a type of martyrdom for the parents when insisting on good moral behavior (i.e. dressing modestly) or setting necessary boundaries that are not cheerfully accepted, but, rather, are met with strong opposition. So you see, we can't always say a cheerful "yes" to everything! In fact, it can be a sin to say yes to our children when that would mean giving them permission to be in situations that would be occasions of sin.

Where parents can sometimes get in trouble is when they see their children suffering and they want to end the suffering NOW--and may even consider doing something to alleviate their child's suffering at the risk of endangering their eternal happiness. No one loves you or your children more than God does. No one wants each of us to be happy more than God does. But His main concern is for our eternal happiness, and He will do anything possible to get souls to Heaven—even if it means a time of suffering here on earth. To be a faithful follower of Christ will, at times, involve suffering— for ourselves and for our loved ones. Suffering is inescapable in this life whether we follow Christ or not. For those away from the Lord, their suffering is useless, usually self-wrought misery caused by their own selfishness and disobedience. God allows suffering because He will bring a greater good out of it. Mary, Seat of Wisdom, could stand at the foot of the Cross and not cry out against that terrible injustice because of Her trust in God and in His Providence; that He would not be allowing this to happen if it were not for the good of everyone. Knowing that the crucifixion was the cost necessary to redeem mankind and open the gates of Heaven, She stood silently by, offered Her sufferings to the Father along with Her Son's and, thus, shared in the work of redemption.

There are times when parents, like Mary, are asked to stand silently by while their children suffer and refrain from interfering with God's plan to use that suffering to help their children draw near to Him. For example, if one of the children would choose to cohabitate or marry outside the Church, and your refusal to condone in words or actions such an arrangement would cause suffering to all involved. There is usually a temptation to just go along with it, not making waves for the sake of keeping the peace or not turning them away from you and the Faith; when, in reality, a strong-but-loving stance would make it clear to all that you believe what you profess, and in order to have peace and joy in this life and the next, it is necessary to put God first. True love is doing what God wills, no matter the consequences. When we do His will, it may cause a stir for a while, but in the end His will is always best for everyone. The same Jesus Who said, "Peace I give you" also said, "I have come to bring fire on the earth, and how I wish it were already kindled! But I have a baptism to undergo, and what constraint I am under until it is completed! Do you think I came to bring peace on earth? No, I tell you, but division. From now on there will be five in one family divided against each other, three against two and two against three. They will be divided, father against son and son against father, mother against daughter and daughter against mother, mother-in-law against daughter-in-law and daughter-in-law against mother-in-law." Luke 12:49-53

This is especially likely to happen in this age when the culture has been de-Christianized and evil is presented as good to our children in varied ways throughout the media. A father of seven told me a few weeks ago that his 18-year-old daughter came home from her first semester of college and told him she was angry with him because he had repressed her sexuality, but now she has found freedom in pornography. Another father told me his college-age son came to him and his wife and said he was homosexual and wanted their approval to bring his boyfriend home with him for visits. The father was against this, the mother wanted to allow it. A woman confided in me that her daughter is in a lesbian relationship and is going to have a baby that the two women will call their own. St. Thomas Aquinas tells us that the highest form of charity is fraternal correction. It is a very difficult thing to do, to speak the truth in love to someone you don't want to offend. Sacred Scripture guides us, "I urge you therefore, brothers, by the mercies of God, to offer your bodies as a living sacrifice, holy and pleasing to God, your spiritual worship. Do not conform yourselves to this age but be transformed by the renewal of your mind, that you may discern what is the will of God, what is good and pleasing and perfect. (Romans 12) May our words and our actions speak loudly the love we have for Christ and His Church, and our desire that everyone obey Him and so find the joy and peace of living in His light-- His truth—His Will.

There is no true, lasting happiness without Jesus, without doing His Will. Loving Jesus brings peace and a deep joy that the world cannot give. So to make your children happy, do all you can to train them to be faithful disciples of our Lord. That means they must know the Faith and love Jesus. I advise you to take the responsibility of teaching your children the Faith. Don't hand that responsibility to others even if you send your children to Catholic schools. God has given you the primary duty of teaching the Faith to your children.

Don't expect the Catholic elementary school, the high school, or the Catholic university to teach it to them. If you don't hand it on to them, chances are they won't learn it or practice it. And what a tragedy that would be, for life lived without putting God in first place is a life filled with sin and sadness. Teach them the commandments, for how can they keep them if they do not know them? Here is an example of a young man who went to Catholic school, yet graduated from high school not knowing the most basic truth of the Faith—the reality, the importance of the Holy Eucharist.

He used to serve Mass frequently at our monastery. He had attended Catholic schools all through high school. One day I saw him as he prepared to serve Mass. He had put on a cassock and was looking at himself in the full-length mirror that hangs in the sacristy. He was discerning the priesthood. I saw him a few years later pushing carts in the parking lot of Lowe's. He told me he had decided to get married and they had a baby; he added that he didn't go to church anymore. I asked him if he knew it was a serious sin to miss Mass on Sundays. He expressed surprise and said no, no one had ever told him that. Mom and Dad, that was your job! They probably taught that in the Catholic schools he attended--at least we hope and pray they did—but, regardless, parents are primarily the ones God will hold accountable for passing on the Faith.

That said, in the culture we live in today, even young people from the best Catholic families sometimes go astray. Those parents who have done their best, have taught the Faith in word and actions, can trust that God will someday, like the father of the Prodigal Son, run to meet their child, embrace him with love and clothe him in a beautiful robe of grace once more.

9

*You live in Me and we are one; you will bear much
fruit and become powerful, because you will
disappear like a drop of water in the ocean.
Within you will pass my silence, My humility, My
purity, My charity, My gentleness, My patience,
My thirst for suffering, My zeal for souls,
to want to save them at any cost.*

Divine Substitution

Blessed Dina Belanger was born in Canada in 1897.
She wrote: "He gave me His spirit in place of my
own; His judgment so that I might appreciate things,
happenings, people in the way He wished. After
that, He replaced my will with His own; then I felt a
great strength which urged me on towards good
and compelled me to refuse Him nothing."

This mystical gift of the exchange of will in her,
Jesus called *Divine Substitution*. This gift consisted
of Jesus substituting Himself for her in such a way,
that she lived the life of Heaven while He lived in
her place on earth. St. John of the Cross said, "The
soul of one who loves God always swims in joy,
always keeps holiday, and is always in the mood for
singing." That sounds like the Divine Substitution
that Bl. Dina Belanger experienced.

Her will had become so united to His that He was
able to freely act in and through her as though she

45

was another humanity for Him to operate in on earth. Sounds so wonderful, doesn't it? Who wouldn't like to live in Heaven while Jesus lived our life on earth? But it is a gift that isn't simply for the asking. It is for those generous souls who ask *and* are willing to do what it takes to die to self in order to be able to receive His great gifts. Oh, to be able to say with St. Paul, "It is no longer I who live, but it is Christ Who lives in me." Bl. Dina Belanger came to understand that Our Lord is *seeking* to bestow such gifts on other generous souls.

Please, Lord, give us generous hearts! Let us marvel at what we have to look forward to as we continue our quest to make of our lives a ceaseless act of love! Heaven on earth—loving God with all our heart, all our mind, all our strength, and all our soul! "to act out of love for Jesus alone; not seeking myself or any created thing." (Bl. Dina Belanger)

Our Lord also revealed to her, "Apart from the eternal and perfect happiness that I enjoy in My Father and in Myself, my happiness is to reproduce Myself in the souls that I created out of love. The more a soul allows Me to reproduce Myself faithfully in her, the more joy and contentment I find. The greatest joy a soul can give Me is to allow Me to raise her up to My Divinity. Yes, my little Bride, I take immense pleasure in transforming a soul into Myself, in deifying it, in absorbing it wholly into the Divinity."

10

Be watchful that the thorns of preoccupations don't suffocate the act of love, and remember that it's through patience that the soul will bear the fruit to which it aspires!

God Alone

St. John of the Cross tells us:

> "Perfection consists in voiding and stripping and purifying the soul of every desire. God will give to the soul a new understanding of God in God, the old human understanding being cast aside-- and a new love of God in God. The soul is wearied and fatigued by its desires... the (desires) disturb it, allowing it not to rest in any place or in any thing whatsoever.... the desires and indulgence in them all cause it greater emptiness and hunger."

The Lord commands us to love God with all our heart, all our mind, all our strength and all our soul. If our heart is filled with desire for things of this world, we leave little room for love of Him Who created us and Who has far more valuable things He desires to give us—things that will make us truly happy in this life and for eternity. What do most people desire? As you would guess, most people desire money, popularity, comfort, good health, beauty, a family, long life, and other good things of this world. Although not evil in themselves, the desire for them can induce sin, such as greed, envy, sloth, and even idolatry, if we desire or love anything more than we desire and love God.

How can desires possibly lead to idolatry? Consider the inordinate attention and honor given those in the world who have achieved fame as actors, singers, sports heroes, etc., regardless of their virtue or lack thereof. They are 'idolized' in our culture. Do you think on Judgment Day God will care how many times one carried a piece of pig skin across a white line on a football field? Or will He care how well known or powerful one was during their life on earth? If you want to know the sort of person God delights in, read the biography of Bl. Margaret of Costello, born blind and lame--her little body badly deformed. She was rejected even by her parents. Not resorting to self-pity, anger or hatred, she lived her life for God and others. She loved God above all, loving and forgiving everyone who had ever hurt her, and they were many. At her funeral, thousands of people came to pay their respects, acclaiming her a saint.

Those who deserve to be loved most and respected most are those who love God most. Normally speaking, we can't tell who those persons are, so we strive—St. John of the Cross tells us—to love all equally.

St. Elizabeth of the Trinity

"A soul that debates within its self, that is taken up with its feelings, and pursues useless thoughts and desires, scatters its forces, for it is not wholly directed toward God... The soul that keeps something for itself in its "inner kingdom," whose powers are not "enclosed" in God, cannot be a perfect praise of glory..."

Servant of God, Fr. John Hardon, tells us "desire what you need, desire what God wants, desire what is right, desire Heaven and the means of reaching Heaven, which is grace. The Promise of having only these desires: your desires will always be satisfied. Happiness is possible only when we conform our desires to the will of God."

11

*Tell all souls that I prefer an act of love
and a Communion of love to
any other gift which they may offer Me.*

The Source of Holiness

Loving Jesus in the Most Blessed Sacrament is at the heart of the ceaseless act of love. Receiving Jesus in Holy Communion with love gives us the power to offer God a continuous effusion of love as we go out from Mass to live the life Jesus created us to live— spreading the Gospel of Love by loving. Jesus Eucharistic is the source through which we receive the grace to love, and the One to Whom we must return in order to obtain the grace to continue to love.

Jesus instructed Sr. Consolata to make a continuous act of love from one Holy Communion to the next. I feel I must clarify what Jesus meant by "Communion," since I asked a good friend--who is not Catholic--to edit this book. She thinks other non-Catholics may be interested in reading it. So to clarify, He was speaking about Holy Communion in the Catholic Church. That is because in the Catholic Church, at Holy Mass, bread and wine are really, truly changed into the Body and Blood of Jesus. The power to effect this miracle comes from God. Jesus gave that power to the Apostles and they passed it on to those on whom they laid their hands and ordained to be presbyters, which means priests. The Catholic Church has maintained Apostolic Succession throughout the centuries—that is, every Catholic Bishop and priest can trace his ordination back to one of the Apostles. They are part of an unbroken chain through which the power has been passed on from Our Lord to His Apostles in order to continue till the end of time what He did at the Last Supper—feed His disciples with His very Self. Some of the Protestant ecclesial communities have communion services, but what they receive is bread and grape juice; for them, it is symbolic. In the Catholic Church it is not symbolic; it is indeed the glorified Body and Blood of Jesus—His Body, Blood, Soul and Divinity. In other words, it is the living, glorified, risen Lord Himself, Who is substantially present in only two places: in Heaven and in the Holy Eucharist. This transubstantiation takes place only through the power of God Who acts through the priest.

In 2003, Pope John Paul II wrote in his encyclical *Ecclesia de Eucharistia*:

> In the Eucharist, "unlike any other sacrament, the mystery [of communion] is so perfect that it brings us to the heights of every good thing: Here is the ultimate goal of every human desire, because here we attain God and God joins himself to us in the most perfect union." Precisely for this reason it is good to *cultivate in our hearts a constant desire for the sacrament of the Eucharist.*

The Church teaches that receiving Jesus in Holy

Communion is the greatest possible union we can have with God here on earth. The great spiritual writer and author of <u>The Spiritual Life</u>, Tanquerey, said that our union with God when we receive Holy Communion is greater than the union of sugar dissolved in hot coffee. St. Faustina prayed, "Lord, *glorify* divinize me by means of the Holy Communion I receive each day." The Eucharist is the perfect prayer, the source and summit of our lives! Jesus said to Bl. Dina Belanger, "My Eucharistic Heart loves to confide in souls, it is like a great need. But I find few pure souls who understand this. To be *close friend* confidante of My intimate secrets, a soul must be very pure, **constantly intent on thinking of and acting for Me alone.**"

The Holy Eucharist is the source of holiness. Our adoration of our Eucharistic Lord and our loving Communions are the source of tremendous graces for ourselves and for every person in the world! One day before her Holy Hour Jesus showed Bl. Dina Belanger a multitude of souls on the precipice of hell. After her Holy Hour, Jesus showed her the same souls in the Hands of God. Jesus told her that through Holy Hours of prayer, a multitude of souls go to Heaven who otherwise would have gone to hell. One person can make up for what is lacking in the lives of others by winning precious efficacious *effective* graces for their salvation.

12

*For your faithfulness to the ceaseless act of love to
become heroic, it is necessary
to will it, strongly will it, heroically will it.*

Where We Will Get the Strength

To make our lives a ceaseless act of love requires
much grace. Our souls are filled with grace at
Baptism. Grace is increased in our souls mostly
through Holy Communion and the other
sacraments. And for those who have lost the life of
grace through serious sin, grace is restored through
the sacrament of confession.

The number of people who undertake this heroic
effort will depend on the grace of God and the
generosity of souls. Some will practice it to a
greater degree than others, but it will benefit
everyone to make use of the act of love as much as
they can. No matter how determined one may be, it
is humanly impossible to make any act of love--let
alone a ceaseless act of love--without the grace of
God. Jesus said that without Him we can do
nothing. He is the source of our strength and our
holiness. How do we get this grace to make
ceaseless acts of love? Jesus implies the answer to
this when He said He wants *a continual act of love
from Communion to Communion.* It is receiving
Jesus in Holy Communion that will give us what is
needed to do all He asks of us. Jesus became man to
redeem us; He rose from the dead in order to stay

with us and communicate to us the graces He gained for us by His death on the Cross. The Eucharist is the primary means by which He distributes those graces. When we receive Holy Communion, we receive not a thing, but a Person— a living Person—the Second Person of the Blessed Trinity: the risen, glorified Jesus. Jesus was present in one place when Mother Mary lovingly placed Him in the manger for the shepherds to adore. Since the Resurrection, Our Risen Lord Jesus is substantially present in only two places: in Heaven and in the Holy Eucharist.

Vatican II tells us that Jesus is present in our souls, in Sacred Scripture, and in one another; but His Presence with us in the Holy Eucharist is the Presence par excellence, because the Eucharist is Jesus Christ Himself. In this Sacrament of sacraments, Jesus is present Body, Blood, Soul and Divinity. Think of it! We actually eat the Body of Jesus! In Scripture, when the Jews heard Jesus say that His Flesh is real food and His Blood is real drink, they were scandalized. Read the passage and imagine hearing this for the first time.

> *I am the bread of life. Your fathers ate the manna in the wilderness and they died. This is the bread which comes down from heaven, that a man may eat of it and not die. I am the living bread which came down from heaven; if any one eats of this bread, he will live for ever; and the bread which I shall give for the life of the world is My Flesh. (John 6:48-51)*

They couldn't believe what they were hearing!

They couldn't imagine eating the flesh of a human being. But Jesus did not retract His statement; He meant what He said, and they knew He meant what He said. Their reply was:

How can this man give us His Flesh to eat?

Jesus replied, "Truly, truly, I say to you, unless you eat the flesh of the Son of man and drink His blood, you have no life in you; he who eats My Flesh and drinks My Blood has eternal life, and I will raise him up at the last day. For My Flesh is food indeed and My Blood is drink indeed. He who eats My Flesh and drinks My Blood abides in Me and I in him. As the living Father sent Me, and I live because of the Father, so he who eats Me will live because of Me. This is the bread come down from heaven, not such as the fathers ate and died; he who eats this bread will live for ever." (John 6:52-59)

After that many of His disciples drew back and no longer went about with Him. (John 6:66)

They could not believe because they did not love. But for those who loved Him, even though they did not understand, their love caused them to trust; they believed Him Who is Truth. Later they would come to understand that it is not the dead flesh of a mere human person that we eat. No. We eat the sacred, divinized flesh of the Second Person of the Blessed Trinity. We eat the glorified, risen Jesus, the flesh God assumed when He became man. We receive a living Person when we receive Holy Communion, and that profound union of a loving

Communion divinizes us!

What does that mean, to be divinized? I heard a priest describe it like this. "Supernatural" means above nature. It would be supernatural for a rock to be able to grow; it would be supernatural for a plant to be able to walk; it would be supernatural for a dog to be able to talk. Imagine you had a pet dog-- we'll call him Banjo--whom you loved very much, and you had the power to share your humanity with him; but you could share your nature with him only to the extent that he obeyed you. Imagine teaching your dog how to talk, how to sit at table and eat with you in a mannerly way, and have a discussion with you.

What God gives us when we become His adopted children through baptism is much, much more than what we could give a pet if we were able to give it a share in our humanity. That would be a creature sharing his nature with another creature. But in baptism, it is the Creator, Almighty God who takes us lowly creatures and shares with us His nature, His divinity. Supernatural grace makes it possible for us to become like God! What a great gift that we too often take for granted. But we should thank God for it every day; for, with it, our actions become more like God's, and this union with God makes it possible for us to enter with Him into eternal happiness. Without supernatural grace, our actions more easily become like beasts and we cannot enter Heaven.

The essence of human nature consists in two points, animality and rationality. Man thus is in a unique position in the universe for he shares in some way the natures of all creatures. His body is material like the rest of the universe; he feeds and grows as an individual, and multiplies as a race like the plants; he perceives with his senses and experiences sense desires like the brute animals: and he even has a share in the angels' nature for he is a rational being, endowed with intellect and will. In a word, he can know and he can love; in this, he even resembles God. But this very complexity of his nature can lead to difficulty, for the animal nature in man has its own knowledge and desire, which may be opposed to, and even anticipate, the decisions of the higher intellectual nature which should rule his actions. And further, this complexity could mean that man's corporal life should come to an end; he is not by nature immortal.

It was in regard to these two points that God showed His goodness, for in the creation of Adam and his help-mate Eve to be the first parents of the human race, God was not satisfied merely with endowing them with perfection of all that human nature called for, but He further added two gifts that were in no way due to it. The first was the privilege of immunity from death; the other was what is called the gift of integrity. To understand this latter gift, one must realize that, as an animal, man has the power of sense knowledge and can experience a desire of what is pleasing to his senses. He can desire food or pleasure; he can be moved to anger, in fact he is subject to all the animal passions. Now this sense life in man pursues its own good, which is by no means always identical with the real good indicated by man's rational faculties. And thus there can arise a conflict in man's own being; as St. Paul puts it: the flesh lusts against the spirit and a difficulty and painful effort may be necessary to assert the due supremacy of reason. Adam and Eve were given a special privilege called "integrity, " by which their reason had complete control over their animal nature; they could not be carried away by sense desire to irrational action, nor could their judgment be blinded by passion. They had complete harmony in due subordination to their higher faculties.

But God's benignity *[Kindness]* was not satisfied even then. God deigned *[(deign) Lower oneself]* to raise him even to a participation in His own divine nature. It is true that this sharing in God's nature does not make man God; man does not share in the divine nature as he shares, say, the animal nature; the change in him produced by this participation is accidental rather than substantial. But man was raised to a supernatural order, and given a life altogether above his natural end or natural powers; he was raised to the state of sanctifying grace.
(*The Tremendous Lover*, M. Eugene Boylan)

You may wonder how the sharing in the divine life of God, supernatural grace, could make such a huge difference in peoples' behavior. You can find examples of Christ-like behavior by reading the lives of the Saints; and, then, compare them to the people you know, and read about those who reject God and His laws. Take, for example, some people who lived in the not-too-distant past and compare their lives. Mother Teresa spent her life serving others. The words she spoke were full of wisdom. Her actions were courageous and generous. She saved a countless number of lives over the years, as she went about the streets of India picking up the abandoned who were left lying in the gutters to die, and sheltering children who had been abandoned and left defenseless. She and her Sisters brought God's love into the lives of millions of people, and even after Mother Teresa's death, her work continues through her community of Sisters, which number in the thousands, and the Missionary of Charity Fathers.

I once visited one of the Missionaries of Charity houses for the dying in Mexico. There were four Sisters there caring for six men who were dying of cancer and other diseases. One of the men, quite tall and who at one time must have been quite handsome, came into the room. He had a large growth on his lower lip, which protruded out about five inches. It was an open wound, repulsive to look at. The Sisters told me that he had been found living on the streets and brought to them by the authorities who asked them to care for him until he died, which they thought would be in a few months. A lovely, very young Sister came out with a bowl and swab to treat the wound. I watched as she tended to this man with great respect and tenderness. Like Mother Teresa, this young Sister-- and who knows how many Sisters now and in the future—is an example of forgetting self and living in the will of God.

Compare Mother Teresa's life with that of someone

addicted to something--whether it be drugs, alcohol, eating too much or too little, shopping, or any number of other things--or a thief, or greedy businessman. People who live their lives just for themselves are like the fig tree Jesus cursed. It looked healthy, but it bore no fruit. And if truth be known, almost all of our lives have some degree of this sort of fruitlessness because of selfishness.

The Saints give us examples of those among us who have been able to rise above our fallen human nature and participate in God's Divine Nature to a degree that produces tremendous fruit. It requires heroic virtue, which requires self-forgetfulness. Some of the Saints give us an image of being like Christ without any extraordinary external manifestations, and others, like St. Pio, had many extraordinary supernatural gifts. In his hands and feet he had the bleeding wounds of Christ: the stigmata. People traveled from all over the world to attend his Mass and go to him for confession. He could read souls and he had the gift of healing and of knowing the future. He could even bi-locate. Some Saints have even raised people from the dead. The gifts are not the reason they were canonized a Saint; they were declared a saint because they believed in Jesus, and they lived lives of heroic virtue. "Very truly I tell you, whoever believes in Me will do the works I have been doing, and they will do even greater things than these, because I am going to the Father. And I will do whatever you ask in My Name, so that the Father may be glorified in the Son. You may ask Me for anything in My Name, and I will do it." (John 14:12-14)

13

*You must have such mastery over your
thoughts and your words that the devil
can't bother you in any way.*

Mystical Bodies

Some of the Fathers of the Church say that there is
not only the Mystical Body of Christ; there is also
the mystical body of satan! The lives of some men
give a hint of that. Adolf Hitler's life brought great
suffering and death to millions of men, women and
children. At the concentration camps that he had
ordered to be built and filled with what he
considered "undesirables," atrocious, demonic
events took place, such as experiments on some of
the people held captive there. I will never forget
one such experiment I read about years ago that
tested many mothers, an unknown number, to
discover how much they would suffer for their
child. They put a mother in one chair and her child
in a nearby chair, so she could see him. On the
mother's chair was a button that, when pressed,
sent an electric current to her child sitting in the
opposite chair. They began with low voltage shocks
to the mother, and gave her the option of taking the
shock herself, or pushing a button that would send
the shock to her child instead. At first the mother
would accept the suffering rather than see her child
suffer.   Then those performing the experiment
would gradually keep increasing the voltage to see

how much suffering the mother would accept before she would push the button, so that she would not receive the shock but her child would. I have questioned myself at times how much suffering would I endure before pushing the button. Knowing my weakness, I shudder at the possibilities.

This morning at Mass I thought about this, and the thought came to me that Jesus had a button, so to speak. The suffering He endured was even more horrific than our human minds can imagine. His pure Body and Soul were extremely sensitive to the evils inflicted upon Him. As God, at any moment He could have "pushed the button" and come down from the Cross. The consequence of never being able to go to Heaven would have been the shock we would have received. Praise God for His infinite love!

Those hideous experiments and other heinous acts at the camps help us realize how depraved we humans are capable of becoming when our fallen human nature is not elevated with God's great gift of sanctifying grace. Thank God for this great gift, and for the other great gift He has given us to restore us to grace if we should lose it by committing serious sin: the gift of confession. Confession not only restores the grace we had lost by sinning, but gives us more grace than if we hadn't sinned! Why? Because of our sorrow that we sinned and our humility in confessing our sins to a priest. Thank You, Lord! Thank You! Thank You! How few would be able to enter Heaven were it not for the gift of confession.

We are commanded not to judge, but to love and to forgive sinners. We are never to judge others in the sense that we think we are superior to them, or say they are going to hell. We can judge actions as being evil, but we cannot judge people, for we do not know their hearts and there, but for the grace of God, go I. It is only by the grace of God and His Divine Providence that I have been baptized, am Catholic, can take advantage of His great gifts of the sacraments, and am in the state of grace. That is why we have the duty, the **duty**, to forgive those who sin against us, for the grace thus gained through our forgiveness will go to the one who offended us and may be the means through which that person is saved. In fact, St. John of the Cross tells us: "Have a great love for those who contradict and fail to love you, for in this way love is begotten in a heart that has no love."

We have the **duty** to pray for the conversion of all sinners. God sanctifies us not just for our own sake, but also for the salvation of others. And the more we love God, the more we will desire the salvation of all souls and the more powerful our prayers become: "The prayer of the righteous is powerful and effective." (James 5:16)

And what peace and joy there is in praying for others rather than getting perturbed over their actions! I used to get quite upset when I went to church and saw things that were out of order. But thanks be to God that is changing. For example, one Saturday afternoon I was out of town and went to the parish church to have some quiet time with the

Lord. I knew there was a wedding that afternoon at 2:00, so I waited till 4:00, thinking confessions began then, so surely the church would be quiet. I was wrong. The wedding party was lined up in front of the altar on the sanctuary steps, not very modestly dressed, making quite a din with their laughter and talking. This went on for quite a while. Meanwhile, I sat in the last pew on the opposite side of the church from the confession line and sang a little tune we sing about the ceaseless act of love....."I will think of everything. You, think only of loving Me. The more that you love Me, the happier that you will be, and every act of love will save a soul. Jesus, Mary, I love You. Save souls." I sang in a normal tone, yet no one could hear me because of the loud noise coming from the wedding party. I was filled with peace as I sang, knowing that my acts of love were bringing light to the situation, and that the reaction I would have had in the past of sadness or getting perturbed would have done no one any good, and possibly would have added to the darkness. I suddenly imagined myself among the growing throng at the scene of the crucifixion who were drowning out the blasphemies and indifference of a countless number of onlookers with our "Jesus, Mary, I love You. Save souls." What peace and joy filled my heart!

The next day the same thing happened again; this time it was after Mass when families came to have their babies baptized. Again I did not feel annoyed, but kept my peace and made acts of love. I'm beginning to see. We must be masters of ourselves, think of no one good or bad, and make ceaseless acts of love. When we do this, we avoid getting angry and judging others; instead, we remain at peace and do good to them! The benefits of the ceaseless act of love are immense for the church, the world, and ourselves.

14

You see, Consolata, sanctity means self-forgetfulness
in everything, in thoughts, desires, words....
Allow Me to do it all! I will do everything;
but you should, at every moment, give Me what I ask
for with much love!

He Leaves Us Free to Choose

This life we are living is a short period of time (compared to eternity) that will determine whether we spend eternity in a place of supreme love and happiness, or a place of supreme hate and misery. This is a time of testing. You may wonder why God would test us. Isn't God love? Wouldn't it be more loving to let everyone go to Heaven? That does sound nice; it would be great if everyone could eventually be in Heaven. But because God is love, only love can get us into the eternal abode of Love—a place where Love permeates everything, where there is no sorrow or pain, only total peace and happiness that is the fruit of perfect love, supernatural love.

The only way to achieve this supernatural love is to make a choice: serve myself, or serve God; do my will, or His. He became a man and showed us what love is; that it is laying down your life for others. It is, as He Himself told us, picking up our cross and following Him to the way of death to self, and life for and in God. That is the cost. It sounds foreboding, doesn't it? Who could do such a thing? The answer is no one, but with God all things are possible. He created us in such a way that we can never find peace and happiness in this world or the next unless we love Him. To love Him is to be willing to pick up that Cross He wants us to carry, and do His will.

If we choose not to follow Him, the world will give us a different cross to carry. We may be tempted to choose the one the world offers because it glitters on the outside, but don't be fooled—it is all misery within. It leads inward to self, where there is a terrible emptiness. Our life becomes a selfish preoccupation of looking for things that will make *me* happy; and, since we are created in the image of God, nothing created can fill that inner void.

The path to happiness in this world and in eternity involves using created things in a manner that fulfills the purpose for which God created them: to fill our hearts with wonder and gratitude, seeing how good God is and how much He loves us in surrounding us with a world filled with beauty and splendor. But all creation cannot possibly satisfy the desire of our heart to love and be loved; we need something greater than ourselves to satiate our deep desire for love and happiness. Created things are good and are meant to lead us to God. Fr. Thomas Dubay writes in <u>The Evidential Power of Beauty</u>, "The acute experience of great beauty readily evokes a nameless yearning for something more than earth can offer." St. John Henry Newman says, "They are echoes from our home." We need something—Someone greater than anything in creation in order to satisfy the longings of our hearts. God created us for a definite purpose: to spend an eternity of love and joy with Him.

He gives us the gift of sharing in the work of our own redemption, and that of others, when we accept the sufferings He allows in our lives and offer them, united with Jesus' sufferings on the Cross, to the Father. Yes, it does entail carrying a cross; but the irony is, the cross, when embraced with love for God, becomes a source of peace and even joy; a peace and a joy that the world cannot give. And oh how sweet it is when one discovers this 'secret' of the joy of surrender!

Jesus told Sr. Consolata:

> *Love Me and you will be happy; and the more you love Me, the happier you will be. Oh, if people loved Me, what joy would reign in the miserable world.*

As we live on earth, so will we live in Heaven. If we love God on earth, we will love Him in Heaven. If God would allow everyone to go to Heaven, even the imperfect, they would be miserable even there; and their presence would prevent Heaven from being perfectly blissful.

One night my college-age nephew came to visit me with his mother, his sister and his girlfriend. My nephew is a very talented singer and pianist. We decided to go across the street so he could play the piano in the Church. It was heavenly as his beautiful voice filled the empty church with songs of praise.   Love for God so filled our hearts as we contemplated the words of love he sang!

Then I thought of a man I know, for whom I pray much, who hasn't stepped foot into a church since he was very young. Most of his life he has been on an artificial high. This man actually mourns over those in his family who are, as he puts it, "so far to the right;" those who love God and are against what he thinks should be our rights, like abortion. Obviously God is not his master. If he had been with us in the church that evening, he would have been uncomfortable and would have wanted to leave. Likewise, someone who had not loved God on earth would not be happy with Him in Heaven, where the essence of all happiness is loving God and being loved by Him--an ecstasy of Love!

God wants everyone to be saved, but it is love that saves us, and to love, one must have free will. Love is to freely choose to deny self and to put God first. Christ said, "If you would be My disciple, you must deny yourself, pick up your cross and follow Me." We live in a culture that is telling us through songs, movies, and all the voices of the world to "Go for the gusto!", that if we break through the social barriers of respect for authority, we will find happiness. But Christians know better; we love Jesus--we have tasted the sweetness of the Lord, and we would rather be on the Cross with Him than be on a cruise without Him! We know that there is no peace, no true joy without Jesus. When we have Him, we have everything.

St. Augustine had this to say about happiness:

"There are two kinds of persons: those who seek their happiness in God, and those who look for it in themselves; the first have the Spirit of the Lord within, the second are dwelling alone. If it is asked why the one are happy, the right answer is because they cleave to God. If it is asked why the others are miserable, the right answer is, because they do not cleave to God. There is no possession that can make any rational or intellectual creature happy except God."

15

*Don't omit a single act of love for Me, see Me in
everyone and say a resolute "yes" to all,
with firm confidence that My help will never fail you.
And smile. Always smile.
I Myself will be smiling through you.*

Prudence Needed

Jesus is saying that a ceaseless act of love consists
not just in making acts of love to Him through
prayer, but it also *must* include acts of love to our
neighbor. Our service can be an act of love when we
see not the person or persons we are serving, but
see Jesus, and do all for love of Jesus. Whether we
have a particular fondness for those we serve or
not, whether we are performing a service we enjoy
or not is of no importance. In fact, good acts that go
against our nature but done for love of God are
more meritorious. This is an act of love: that no
matter who it is we are asked to serve, or what it is
we are asked to do (sin excluded), we do it willingly
with love for Jesus, with a sweet smile.

Jesus said to say a resolute "yes" to all. But of
course that is not a blanket statement true in all
circumstances. He clarifies that we say "yes" unless
it interferes with our duties or goes against charity.
For example, a wife and mother should not neglect
her family responsibilities or go against her
husband's wishes by assenting to requests to help

others with the reasoning, "Jesus said to say 'yes' to all." Duty and charity come first.

In the book, <u>Mystical City of God</u> by Ven. Mother Mary Agreda, there is a scene in the life of the Blessed Virgin Mary where the devil would occasionally send a woman to knock on Mary's door to try to engage Mary in conversation in order to take her away from her contemplative life of silence and prayer. Mary, Seat of Wisdom, would politely greet her, politely dismiss her, and return to her prayer and duties.

16

I want the love of My creatures; and once they love Me, they won't offend Me anymore.

A Test of Love

Like the angels, we must have a test. The fallen angels' sin was pride and disobedience.

It would be wrong to imagine that the immediate condemnation of the rebellious angels, with- out any further time or reconsideration and repentance, is any reflection on God's mercy. The very excellence of the powers of the angelic mind is such, that reconsideration, as we understand it, is meaningless for them. They were in full possession of the facts of the case, completely undisturbed in their judgment by any earthly passions or by lack of reflection, and they saw their obligations and the heinousness of their crime with a clarity that is far beyond anything we can imagine. No amount of time for reconsideration would lead to a reversal of their decision. By their sin they lost the happiness of heaven and became subject to the unspeakable torments of hell. This involved the fearful pain of the loss of God, of the loss of all power to love God or even to love anything else; and that was coupled with the clear knowledge that only in loving God could they find happiness, and that their own free act had made that love impossible forever. Their hatred for God and for all that belonged to Him, was then unspeakable; when they saw the beginning of His plan to create the human race and to raise its members to the exalted positions which they themselves had lost, their fury knew no bounds. From that moment, no effort would be spared by these mighty intelligences to destroy the human race. (*The Tremendous Lover, M. Eugene Boylan*)

The early Church Fathers said that satan fell when God manifested to the angels His plan to become man, born of a virgin. Satan and those who followed him were too proud to serve God looking like a species beneath him in dignity—not nearly as magnificent a creature as an angel! A human being is composed of body and spirit, slow to understand and inclined to do evil. Some of the angels would not bow down and adore God looking like a mere man. St. Michael and the others, even with their great intelligence, did not understand completely this great mystery of the Incarnation, but they humbly fell to their knees and worshipped the God-man. This was the test of the angels; many failed due to their pride. The price of that sin was that they were cast into hell for all eternity. Now they bear great hatred for God and man. This hatred drives them to get as many of us to hell as they can.

Our test is similar to that of the angels. At the Last Supper Christ took bread and said, "This is My Body." He took wine and said, "This is My Blood." Ever since then, God dwells among us under the appearance of bread--a species far beneath us--bread! An inanimate object! He looks like a piece of bread. The proud will not accept His words when He tells us in Sacred Scripture that He is the Bread from Heaven and whoever eats His Body and drinks His Blood will live forever. His humble, faithful followers, not fully understanding this Sacred Mystery, like St. Michael, fall on their knees and worship our Eucharistic Lord.

St. Thomas Aquinas said that, because satan loves power, God chooses to overcome satan not with power, but with weakness: Jesus hanging dead on the Cross; Jesus in the Holy Eucharist. What could appear weaker? It is love and humility that triumphs over evil. How this must confound satan! Humble adoration of God with us in the Holy Eucharist brings down torrents of grace upon the world. It brings light and weakens satan's power. The more who lovingly adore, the more satan is weakened. Mankind's humble adoration of God with us in the Holy Eucharist will be the weight that crushes the head of satan.

So in striving to make our lives a ceaseless act of love, we must guard against the idea that Our Lord wants this act of love--"Jesus, Mary, I love You. Save souls"-- to the exclusion of other prayers, like the Holy Mass, Adoration of Our Eucharistic Lord, and the Holy Rosary. No. The Holy Mass and Adoration and receiving Jesus in Holy Communion are the greatest acts of love we can make; and, if possible, we should do so daily. At Fatima, Our Lady said that the Rosary is the greatest weapon against satan, and She asked us to pray it every day, with family if possible. The Holy Eucharist is the source of holiness. The more we love and adore Our

Eucharistic Lord, the more grace we receive and the more souls we save. The Eucharist is Jesus, the source of holiness; receiving Him with love in Holy Communion is the greatest union with God possible on earth. The acts of love outside of adoration and Mass are the means to continue to adore Our Lord, to save souls, and to receive great graces.

17

*Remember that an act of love on your part can decide
the salvation of a soul, its eternal salvation.
So see that you don't waste a single "Jesus, Mary,
I love You. Save souls!"*

*"Jesus, Mary, I love You. Save souls!" includes
everything: the souls in purgatory,
as well as those in the militant Church;
the innocent soul, as well as the guilty one, the dying
one, the atheist, etc. all souls.*

An Ardent Effusion of Love

*Love is holiness. The more you love Me,
the holier you will become.
Remember that it is love, and love alone, that will
carry you, victorious, to every summit.*

"Our act of love can be set in a formula at certain times, as Jesus said; but it is not to be a mechanical repetition of the formula. A ceaseless act of love must be a continuous, silent, and ardent effusion of love and charity. Insofar as what Jesus wants from us, it's not the number of acts of love that is most important. Between two people, if the former makes a thousand successive acts of love, or nearly that many, and the latter makes a lesser number, but slips them into every free moment of the day, and remains closely united to Jesus, then it's the latter person who will have better understood the Little Way of Love." (The Littlest Way of Love, Part II)

The storm clouds are gathering. It is getting very dark, and imminent chastisement looms over us. Why would a loving God send chastisements? Because He is merciful. In Noah's day, during the time of the great flood, there was much darkness in the world also. If God had not sent the flood, the sin would have continued; and souls, so many souls, would have been lost for eternity. But because of the flood, many cried out to God before they died and were saved. God's love for us impels Him to do whatever is necessary to save our souls. He is a good, merciful Father Who longs for our love, He longs for us to spend eternity with Him in unimaginable bliss. After all, He paid a terrible price for our salvation: the blood of His only begotten Son.

We are given a lifetime during which each of us will either add to the light, or we will add to the darkness. Each thought, each word, and each action will either make this world more like Heaven, or more like hell. Pondering the messages Jesus gave to Sr. Consolata will help us become more aware of the thoughts that enter our minds and the words that come out of our mouths. Scripture tells us that the just man falls seven times a day. When those of us who are trying to love God and do good find that we have failed in some way in our efforts, not to worry! The Lord can use even our failures to add light to the world—more light than if we hadn't failed. When we sin, repent, and humbly confess our sins to a priest, we can receive more grace than if we hadn't sinned.

In fact, that is one reason He allows us to sin, so that, after repenting, we can love Him more than if we hadn't sinned at all. He said to Simon as Mary bathed His feet with her tears, "Her many sins are forgiven because she has loved much."

God the Father told St. Catherine of Siena,

> "Sometimes I allow the world to show them (souls) what it is, so that, feeling its diverse and various passions, they may know how little stability it has, and may come to lift their desire beyond it, and seek their native country, which is the Eternal Life. And so I draw them by these, and by many other ways, for the eye cannot see, nor the tongue relate, nor the heart think, how many are the roads and ways which I use, through love alone, to lead them back to grace, so that my truth may be fulfilled in them. I am constrained to do so by that inestimable love of Mine, by which I created them..." (Dialogue of St. Catherine of Siena)

I think most of us realize that there is much sin in the world and in the Church today. The Body of Christ is suffering greatly; She is very weak. Perhaps what adds most to the darkness are not the sins of unbelievers, but those of Christians who live with a terrible indifference towards God, and, towards the fact that His Son is dwelling among us in the Holy Eucharist. In these days, many have no sense of sin. They reject, in their actions if not in words, some of the Church's teachings. To reject one of the official teachings of the Church is to reject the Catholic Faith. "To lose the faith, it is not necessary to believe nothing: it is enough not to believe one sole article; it is even enough to doubt it. Do you hesitate to believe in indulgences or in purgatory? When you would give your life for all the other truths, you would die unfaithful, and you would be martyr only of your own sentiments." (St. John of the Cross)

Thomas Dubay says this about the Church:

"Despite the sinfulness of some of her members, She (the Church) remains the home of the saints, *the people who embrace her teaching without selectivity and live it to the hilt.* They are the beautiful ones who show why the Church is the home of delight, a transforming delight – which is what her mystics are mainly about: our destiny and how to get there."

Let us be among those who fulfill the destiny for greatness for which God created us. He is worthy to be loved above all else. Always remember His infinite love for us that compelled Him to endure the greatest agony ever suffered, and to shed every drop of His Blood so that *we* would not have to suffer, but could spend an eternity of unimaginable happiness with Him.

Our Lord's Passion "was a short time as measured by movement of the sun; but if measured as moments of pain are really measured, by the intensity of agony, those few hours were longer than the whole duration of the world. For we cannot conceive what our Lord endured in those hours. His body was designed for suffering, and the power of His divinity was used only to avoid the remedy that human weakness would otherwise have found, that of loss of consciousness, and even of life, through sheer pain. No human being ever suffered as our Lord suffered in that physical agony, and the physical agony was a mere drop in the ocean compared with the exquisite agony of His mind and heart. For the heart of the Crucified burned with a more intense love of God than the world has ever known, and the Son's heart was torn by the offences that men offer to His heavenly Father. And in the same heart there was a fire of love for men, of love for each man and for every man, and the Lover's heart was torn by the thought of the coldness of those whom He loved and the loss they were incurring by their refusal to love Him. On the Cross that love wrings every drop of blood from His divine heart. Truly we must call Him, "This Tremendous Lover." (*This Tremendous Lover*, M. Eugene Boylan)

The other day one of our Sisters said that Jesus tells us to think only of Him. He asks only what He Himself does for us, for if He forgot us for even an instant, we would fail to exist. Another Sister said that He asks us to think only of loving Him, as He thinks only of loving us as He awaits us in the tabernacle to come and love Him, to return love for Love. Oh how I thank God for my Sisters! What great graces He has given these beautiful young souls!

18

I desire a continuous act of love
from one Communion to another.

It is the Lord!

The Holy Mass is the highest form of praise, the perfect prayer. It is perfect, because it is an act of God: it is Jesus offering Himself to the Father. Even if the music is not great or the sermon is not so interesting, it is still the perfect prayer; it is the offering the Son of God makes of His life to God the Father. Good music and inspiring sermons are good things and can help us lift our hearts to God, but they are not essential to worship. When Jesus went to the temple to worship His Father, He did not do so with the expectation of being entertained—to hear beautiful music or hear good sermons. He went to worship, and to worship is to cease self-seeking and focus on pleasing the One we come to adore. That should be our incentive when we attend Mass—to unite our lives with Christ's and offer our lives with His to our Heavenly Father. If everyone in the congregation would come with that intent and participate fully in the Mass, praying from the heart and joining in the prayers and hymns, the music would be out of this world! That is what Vatican II meant by active participation in the Mass: everyone present participating with mind and heart.

It's all about God! It is a time to make a total

surrender of love to Him Who created us and keeps us in existence. Sadly, too few know the true value of the Mass; and some abandon the Faith, not because of a sincere search for truth, but to satisfy the senses--to hear beautiful music, make friends, and feel good about themselves. Even worse, some stay home and watch some preacher or devotion on TV or the computer. They don't understand that the Mass is the perfect prayer. In the Holy Sacrifice of the Mass, we stand at the foot of the Cross, offering our lives to the Father. We worship the Lamb Who was slain, and then go to the Banquet Table and receive as Food the Divine Lamb of God! We receive His Sacred, glorified, divinized Body and Blood. Any worship service outside of the Mass, even with the best music and the best preaching, cannot begin to compare with the abundant graces that are given by devoutly attending Holy Mass. The Mass is the perfect prayer; it is an act of God.

Mass is the greatest thing that happens on earth. It is essential to our spiritual life and essential to maintain our union with God and be prepared to see the Face of God at whatever moment He may call us Home. That is why Church law requires us to attend Mass every Sunday and all Holy Days of obligation. To miss Mass without just cause is a mortal sin. I heard someone once describe a person in mortal sin as a walking spiritual skeleton. The word "mortal" means deadly. Some disregard this law and go to Mass not at all or only occasionally.

There are some who go to Mass regularly, but do not go regularly to confession. In spite of that, almost everyone attending Mass goes to Holy

Communion. To receive Jesus in Holy Communion and benefit by it, we must be in the state of grace. To go to Holy Communion not in the state of grace is to commit another mortal sin; it is a sacrilegious Communion--a great evil. Read what St. Cyril, one of the early Church Fathers, said about it:

> "They who make a sacrilegious Communion receive satan and Jesus Christ into their hearts: satan, that they may let him rule, and Jesus Christ, that they may offer Him in sacrifice as a Victim to satan." (St. Cyril 313-386 AD)

Strong words. It helps us understand why it is a mortal sin to receive Jesus in Holy Communion when we are not in the state of grace.

The Knights of Columbus, in the summer of 2015, took a poll of Catholics that included a question about the Real Presence of Jesus in the Holy Eucharist. Sixty-four percent (64%) of non-practicing Catholics said it is just "a symbol." Only sixty-five percent (65%) of practicing Catholics said the Eucharist is the true presence of Jesus Christ. What a terrible sadness! Thirty-five percent (35%) of practicing Catholics, those who go to Mass and receive Our Lord in Holy Communion, either don't know about, or reject the Church's teaching on this essential matter--the source and summit of our Faith. The Eucharist is the heart of our Faith; it is the Heart of God. It is what makes our Faith worth living and dying for. Every practicing Catholic should be able to say with all their heart, and be ready to prove it with their actions: "My Jesus, I love You above all things. I believe that what I receive in Holy Communion is Your Body, Blood, Soul and Divinity, the living God Incarnate. I believe it because You have said it, and I am willing to give my life to maintain this truth." (Prayer after Communion in the prayer book of Children of Mary)

There are those who reject the Church's teaching; and there are others who simply do not know what the Church teaches. Some were never taught, and some who heard but did not listen. Once I attended Mass at a local parish. Two little girls were altar servers. This particular parish had perpetual adoration so, at the end of the Mass, Father enthroned Our Eucharistic Lord on the altar and he and the girls left the Sanctuary. Then the girls came out of the sacristy and kind of trotted past the altar---without stopping to genuflect or bow to Our Lord, Who was solemnly enthroned there. I felt a nudge from the Lord to go out and talk to them. So I went into the main church and went up to them and said, "Girls, what a privilege that you were able to serve Mass! Was this your first time?" They said no, it was their second time. After a little chit chat, I asked, "Who is it you receive when you go to Holy Communion?" Without hesitation they responded, "The Body and Blood of Jesus." I replied, "Yes! That's right, the Body and Blood of Jesus! Now, is it His dead flesh we eat? Or is it living flesh? Is it the living Jesus? Is it a symbol?" They stopped, looked up to the right, and said slowly, "I guess it's a symbol."

I have had this conversation many times with Catholics of all ages, from teenagers who have gone to Catholic schools all their lives to older people who go to daily Mass; and, sadly, the vast majority have replied as those little girls did.

But the good news is the end of the story. After their response, "I guess it is a symbol," I said with much joy, "I have great news for you! It's not a symbol, its Jesus, the living God! And He loves you more than you can imagine, and He *longs* for you to love Him. He told St. Margaret Mary that He thirsts to be loved in the Most Blessed Sacrament. And you know what? He is in that chapel on the altar right now and I bet He is saying, 'Hurry up and let them come to Me!' (They were listening very intently.) Why don't you go back into the chapel and get down on your knees and tell Jesus you love Him. That will make Him so happy! Those are His favorite words to hear, 'I love you.'" With big smiles on their faces they left immediately and hurried back to love Jesus. I could almost see Him smiling!

Those who have a deeper understanding of Jesus' Presence in the Eucharist are usually those who had been taught the Faith at home. It is very difficult for teachers to teach the Faith to children whose families don't love and practice it. For those children, no matter how many times the teacher presents the truths of the Faith to them, they find it almost impossible to integrate it as truth, because actions speak louder than words.

Imagine what it's like for children whose parents don't know the Faith, don't practice it, and don't communicate by their actions that they love Jesus. When these children do go to church, they see people line up with outstretched hands and receive a white circular piece of bread and walk away as they put this "bread" into their mouths. In the children's minds, do they subconsciously register statements like: The teacher told us this bread is Jesus, and Jesus is God. No one acts like this is God. It can't be true. Nobody talks about it, and they don't even seem to care that God is in that gold box they call a tabernacle. How can it be God if no one talks about Him at home and no one is acting like it is God?

May the Lord pour out His Spirit upon us and fill our hearts with great love for Jesus so that we will love Him above all things and receive Him in Holy Communion every day, if possible, even if it is at a cost. St. Pio said that, if we knew what the Mass really is, we would be willing to risk our lives to attend just one Mass. St. Juan Diego walked fifteen miles to attend Mass every day. I heard a priest tell a story once. It was about a man named Joe who started going to daily Mass. His friend Tom came up to him and said, "Joe, what a good guy you are! You go to Mass every day!" Joe replied, "It's not that I'm a good guy. If Walmart were giving away a thousand dollars every day, would you go? Well, at Mass I get *infinitely* more than a thousand dollars!"

To live one's life around the Holy Mass is a great grace, the wisdom to order this earthly life around what is most important. I have a hunch that, at the moment we stand before St. Peter at the pearly gates, we will be given a deep understanding of the value of the Mass; and one of our greatest regrets will be that we didn't attend Holy Mass as often as we could have. "The celebration of Holy Mass is as valuable as the death of Jesus on the Cross" (St. Thomas Aquinas)

19

Consolata, tell souls that I prefer an act of love, and a Communion of love over any other gift they could offer Me.

Needed: A Revolution of Love for Our Eucharistic Lord

If the Faith is to be passed on and spread throughout the world, we need to treat Our Eucharistic Lord with a reverence born out of a profound love for Him and a sense of awe in His Sacred Presence. As things are now, our actions are contradicting our words. We say it is Jesus: His Body, Blood, Soul and Divinity, but our actions don't communicate that we believe we are receiving God. I am going to write something now that I had not intended to write. I believe the Lord wants it; I'll tell you why. I have told the Lord many times over the years that I will do anything He asks, if He will just let me know what His Will is. The way He normally assures me of His Will is by manifesting it in three ways. During these past few days, the following three things have happened:

1. A priest told me that last year seven consecrated Hosts were found in various places in the church. Aghast, I thought, "if they have found seven Hosts in the church of this rather small parish, how many

times have such travesties occurred in other churches around the country and around the world?!"

2. I was told that a few years ago in a small church in a rural setting, a woman walked up to the priest--visibly shaken and holding a white cloth. She said, "Father, I have Jesus." She explained that her uncle had just told her that he went to Communion at his relative's funeral, but he knew he shouldn't receive, so he took the Host home and put it in a Bible. He had another One somewhere in the house that he had taken from the church three years ago, but he couldn't remember where he had put It. The priest told the woman to go back and tell him that he (the priest) would not eat again until the Host was found and returned. Later that day the Host was returned.

3. A Sister from Pennsylvania sent me a link to a site that told about the Papal Mass in the Philippines in 2014. There I read, "So many people (7-8 million) presented themselves for Communion that it was a logistical impossibility to distribute It to all of them in an orderly fashion. Instead, Hosts were passed hand-to-hand, overhead, through the crowds. How many fragments were lost to be crushed underfoot? How many whole Hosts were stepped on in the mud?"

A few weeks after the priest had told me privately about the desecrations--the seven Hosts being found in his parish church--he informed the entire parish of it during the homily of each of the Masses one Sunday. They were informed, though not in these words, of the reality, that the living God Incarnate, Jesus Eucharistic, had been treated with great irreverence and terrible distain in their parish by some who pretended to receive Him in Holy Communion and who then put Him under a statue, on the floor, or in a missalette. That day, after Mass, the people left the church as usual, greeting one another as they filed out, laughing and talking as if nothing of any importance had just been revealed to them. I sat in the pew and wept.

Currently in the news at that time was the release of videos that revealed that Planned Parenthood was selling body parts from aborted babies. The next day after Mass I was praying ardently that Planned Parenthood would be defunded—that our tax dollars would no longer be spent to subsidize this evil business. Then I heard in my heart these words: "The hidden human life in the womb will not be acknowledged until the hidden Divine life in the Eucharist is acknowledged." The following day after Mass I heard, "Start a movement to restore the law of the Church." I understood immediately that the law referred to was the law concerning receiving Jesus in Holy Communion on the tongue.

Now I have a dilemma. I believe the Lord instructed me to "start a movement to restore the law of the Church". But the USCCB (United States Conference of Catholic Bishops) has said that in the United States, the manner of receiving Holy Communion is to stand and receive on the hand. I am a faithful daughter of the Church; I know that the Holy Spirit guides *the Church* infallibly in matters of Faith and morals--*not me*. Wanting to be true to the Church and to discern if what I understood was indeed from Our Lord, I must do two things: first, determine if what I think the Lord is asking of me is opposed to either Scripture or the teachings of the Church; I know the Lord would never ask me or anyone to go against Sacred Scripture or the teachings of the Church. If what I feel called to do is against the teachings of the Church, that's the end of the story. I will not act on it. But if it does *not* go against the teachings of the Church, then, the second thing I will do is seek guidance from a wise man, as Scripture instructs us to do, to see how I should proceed. So, first let's do some research.

On August 15, 2015, the Bishop of the Diocese of Oruro, Bolivia, declared that he will no longer permit Communion in the hand. The report said that the Bishop, the Polish Verbite missionary Krzysztof (Cristobal) Białasik, made this decision after it was noticed that some people receive the Host but do not consume It, apparently wishing to carry It away for unknown reasons.

In the United States, too, "each bishop may, according to his prudent judgment and conscience, authorize in his diocese the introduction of the new rite for giving communion." So each bishop may or may not allow the practice of Communion in the hand; he decides if this is good for his local Church or not.

The law of the Church is to distribute Holy

Communion on the tongue. To receive in the hand is the result of an indult, an exception from the law that the bishops of some countries requested. Here is an excerpt from the Vatican document granting the indult to the U.S. to allow Holy Communion to be distributed in the hand.

"In reply to the request of your conference of bishops regarding permission to give communion by placing the host on the hand of the faithful, I wish to communicate the following. Pope Paul VI calls attention to the purpose of the Instruction *Memoriale Domini* of 29 May 1969, on retaining the traditional practice in use. (Memoriale Domini recommends Communion on the tongue.) At the same time he has taken into account the reasons given to support your request and the outcome of the vote taken on this matter. The Pope grants that throughout the territory of your conference, each bishop may, according to his prudent judgment and conscience, authorize in his diocese the introduction of the new rite for giving communion. The condition is the complete avoidance of any cause for the faithful to be shocked and any danger of irreverence toward the Eucharist."

There is a bishop, Bishop Athanasius Schneider in Kazakhstan, who travels the world trying to restore reverence to Our Eucharistic Lord. This is what he wrote:

"Unfortunately in the last forty, fifty years, it was spread, a manner to receive and distribute Holy

Communion, called, "in the hand," which really is a cause, an effective cause of the diminishing of the conscience and the faith that it is the Lord. When I can handle the Host as in a very similar manner as I can handle a chip and take with my two fingers and put in my mouth — the same gestures as communion in the hand ..."

Cardinal Antonio Canizares Llovera, former prefect of the Vatican's Congregation for Divine Worship and the Discipline of the Sacraments, now archbishop of Valencia, Spain, in an interview with CNA during his visit to Lima, Peru, recommended that Catholics receive Communion on the tongue, while kneeling. "It is to simply know that we are before God Himself and that He came to us and that we are undeserving. Receiving Communion in this way is the sign of adoration that needs to be recovered. I think the entire Church needs to receive Communion while kneeling."

Many Lutheran congregations receive communion kneeling and on the tongue. Luther did not deny the Real Presence. He had the notion that by the pastor declaring the bread and wine to be the body and blood of Christ, so it was, similar to when John the Baptist declared Jesus to be the Lamb of God. Because Luther believed it was Christ's real presence, he instructed his followers to kneel and receive on the tongue. Calvin, on the other hand, denied the Real Presence of Jesus in the Eucharist and wanted his followers not to kneel, lest anyone see and think they were reverencing what they received. He wanted them to stand and receive in the hand. (see J. R. Luth, "Communion in the

Churches of the Dutch Reformation to the Present Day")

A Lutheran convert wrote, "When I was Lutheran, when I went to communion I was receiving bread. As a Lutheran I received bread kneeling and on the tongue. Now I am Catholic and receive Our Lord Jesus standing and in the hand."

This man now realizes that what he was receiving in the Protestant church was bread. When Catholic priests celebrate Mass, Christ becomes present because they are validly ordained. That is, Catholic priests are ordained by a bishop who can trace his ordination back to one of the Apostles—the Apostles who received from Christ Himself the power to change bread and wine into the Body, Blood, Soul and Divinity of Christ, the power to forgive sins, and to administer all of the sacraments. This is called Apostolic Succession, which Christ intended for His Church so that not only the Apostles could eat His Body and drink His Blood, but every faithful member of His Holy Church could receive this Sacred Food until the end of time.

Yes, what we receive is sacred; it is the Lord. To kneel and receive on the tongue is a more appropriate way of communicating nonverbally that we believe what we profess. In addition, Communion on the tongue is also important for another reason. Bishop Schneider continues:

"...the most grievous aspect in this manner (Communion in the hand) is that the loss of numerous fragments of the Hosts, because they fall down, continuously – no one can deny this. It is a fact. Or they stick on the palms, or the fingers. And then they fall down on earth, and then trampled. <u>Our Lord is *trampled* by His faithful in numerous churches. And we continue quietly, and no one shouts!"</u>

After I read what he wrote, I wanted to shout, with tears in my eyes, "Stop! Please, Dear Lord, let it stop..."

Many years ago I used to receive Holy Communion in the hand. Then I read--I can't recall where--that this is not pleasing to the Lord. Shortly after that I found out that the Holy Father, Pope John Paul II, would not distribute Communion in the hand, but only on the tongue. During this same time period, I was told that Mother Teresa and her Sisters did not receive Communion in the hand, and that it was in their constitutions that they receive only on the tongue. What Fr. Rutler tells in his homily below is cause for reflection.

Father George William Rutler, in a homily on Good Friday, 1989, said:

"I will tell you a secret, since we have just a thousand close friends together, and also because we have the Missionaries of Charity with us, whom the Holy Spirit has sent into the world that the secrets of many hearts might be revealed. Not very long ago I said Mass and preached for their Mother, Mother Teresa of Calcutta, and after breakfast we spent quite a long time talking in a little room. Suddenly, I found myself asking her (I don't know why): 'Mother, what do you think is the worst problem in the world today?'

She more than anyone could name any number of candidates: famine, plague, disease, the breakdown of the family, rebellion against God, the corruption of the media, world debt, nuclear threat, and so on. Without pausing a second she said: 'Wherever I go in the whole world, the thing that makes me the saddest is watching people receive Communion in the hand.'"

I make the assumption that everyone reading this loves Jesus and receives Him in Holy Communion with much reverence. My intent is not to criticize anyone. I have a very dear friend who loves Our Lord. She receives in the hand. When I discussed this matter with her, she told me why she receives in the hand. With tears of love in her eyes, she told me how she looks at Our Eucharistic Lord in her hand, and thinks how humble He is, to come to her. So I in no way question the love of those who receive in the hand. In fact, most people under sixty-five years old were not taught any way other than how to receive in the hand, and so most have no idea that the law of the Church is to receive our Lord on the tongue.

I feel compelled to say out of love for Jesus Eucharistic—the One to Whom my Sisters and I have given our lives—that, because of Communion in the hand, many profanations of the Holy Eucharist are taking place in many places on a regular basis. For example, not out of disrespect, but because of lack of instruction, many do not know that when Holy Communion is received in the hand Sacred Particles are very often, if not always or most of the time, left in the hand after picking up the Host. Some of the Particles fall to the ground, and Our Eucharistic Lord is being trampled upon. I never knew that; no one had ever told me. It wasn't until I read what Mother Teresa said that I checked my hand after receiving Communion; and, to my surprise, I did see Particles of the Host, small Sacred Particles—Jesus! I consumed the Particles and from then on I have received on the tongue.

God revealed to St. Catherine of Siena:

> "You cannot receive the Body without the Blood, or the Blood or the Body without the soul of the Incarnate Word; nor the soul nor the Body without the Divinity of the Eternal God, because none of these can be separated from each other...you receive the whole Divine Essence in that most sweet Sacrament concealed under the whiteness of the bread; for as the sun cannot be divided into light, heat and color, the whole of God and the whole of man cannot be separated under the white mantle of the Host; for even if the Host should be divided into a million particles, in each particle should I be present, whole God and whole man. When you break a mirror, the reflection to be seen in it is not broken; similarly, when the Host is divided God and man are not divided, but remain in each particle. Nor is the Sacrament diminished in itself..."

This is a quote from Bishop Juan Rodolfo Laise of San Luis, Argentina.

> "With Communion in the hand, a miracle would be required during each distribution of Communion to avoid some Particles from falling to the ground or remaining in the hand of the faithful.... Let us speak clearly: whoever receives Communion in the mouth not only follows exactly the tradition handed down but also the wish expressed by the last Popes and thus avoids placing himself in the occasion of committing a sin by negligently dropping a fragment of the Body of Christ."

Some ask how it could be that Mother Teresa was more saddened by Communion in the hand than other tragedies occurring in the world. Whether this sorrow was because she believed the Faith of the people was being weakened by this practice, or because she realized that Sacred Particles were being trampled upon, or because some are not consuming the Host but carrying Our Lord out to who knows where and for what purposes, we do not know; but shouldn't every Catholic—members of the true Faith which Christ established and gave the great gift of Himself in the Holy Eucharist—share in such sorrow for these things?

St. Leo the Great preached:

> "Blessed are they who mourn, for they shall be comforted. But the mourning for which he promises eternal consolation, dearly beloved, has nothing to do with ordinary worldly distress; for

the tears which have their origin in the sorrow common to all mankind do not make anyone blessed. There is another reason for the sighs of the saints, another reason for their blessed tears. Religious grief mourns for sin, one's own or another's; it does not lament because of what happens as a result of God's justice, but because of what is done by human malice."

God became man so He could die and redeem us; He chose to rise from the dead so He could stay with us in His glorified humanity in the Holy Eucharist to communicate to us the graces He had won for us on Calvary. Those graces are ours primarily through our loving reception of Jesus in the Holy Eucharist. He stays with us as the most vulnerable Person on earth, entrusting Himself and His care into the hands of His creatures.

God is omnipotent; but there is something He cannot do, and that is to give us a greater gift than He has given us in the Holy Eucharist. The Eucharist is Jesus, the Food that divinizes us. This is the greatest gift He could give us, and the greatest gift we can give Him is a loving Communion and a ceaseless act of love from Communion to Communion.

What is a loving Communion? Obviously it is to receive Jesus in Holy Communion in a state of grace and with a loving heart, and in a way that is most pleasing to Him. It is the law of the Church to receive Holy Communion on the tongue. From the documents of the Church, it is stated clearly that it is the preferred method of the Church.

Bishop Athanasius Schneider states:

> "And so it was my intention to shout in the Church that bishops and faithful and priests may awaken and recognize that this little, little Host during the distribution of Holy Communion is the Lord! The Creator of Heaven and Earth! The Infinite Majesty and Sanctity of God! Hidden in this, this little Host."

Jesus told St. Margaret Mary, "I thirst. I so thirst to be loved by men in the Most Blessed Sacrament that this thirst devours Me."

**Yes, Lord, let's start a movement to quench
Your thirst for love.
It will be a movement of prayer!
It will be a movement of LOVE!**

Most Holy Trinity, I adore You!

*My God, my God, I love You
in the Most Blessed Sacrament!*

20

*Yes, ask forgiveness for poor guilty humanity,
ask for the triumph of My Mercy for them,
but especially, ask, Oh**! Ask for an outpouring upon
them of the embrace of divine Love which,
like a new Pentecost,
delivers mankind from its illnesses.***

There are Two Liftings

Several years ago I was making a novena to St. Margaret Mary, asking her to obtain for me the grace to understand more deeply devotion to the Sacred Heart of Jesus.   During the days of that novena, I read in a Catholic newspaper that United Way was threatening not to fund the boy scouts because of their stance against homosexual men being leaders of their troops.   Another day I read that a little six-year-old girl in California drowned her three-year-old brother in a mud puddle. I went to chapel deeply disturbed. I prayed, "Lord, I know you overcame sin and death. But why, then, Lord, is there still so much evil in the world? You are Truth Itself, and I believe what You tell us in Scripture: that You overcame sin and death." Then, as I fell to my knees before Him Who was enthroned on the altar, I heard clearly, interiorly, "BY THE BLOOD OF THE CROSS." Then I felt as if a huge computer was trying to download information into my mind, which was being stretched to its limits. What was 'downloaded' I pondered almost every waking moment of the day for the next year. When I finally tried to put it in writing, it came out something like this: There are two liftings. The first was on the throne of the Cross. The second is in the throne of the monstrance. God did His part in the first lifting by shedding every drop of His Blood for us. Now the time has come for the second lifting: for us to do our part by enthroning His Living Sacred Heart—Our Eucharistic Lord--in the monstrance and adoring Him, surrendering all to Him. When we do, the head of satan will be crushed, as the embrace of His divine Love delivers mankind from its illnesses. "When I am lifted up from the earth, I will draw all men to Myself." (John 12:32).

Pray mankind will wake up and see the marvelous work of the Lord in remaining on earth with us in the Most Blessed Sacrament! What terrible indifference exists even within the Church regarding this greatest gift that God has given us. Jesus said to St. Margaret Mary that this great indifference concerning His Presence with us in the Blessed Sacrament made Him suffer more than anything else during His Passion. We need to beg forgiveness for our brothers and sisters throughout the world who do not love and adore Him, who are indifferent towards Him Who dwells with us in the Holy Eucharist. Lord, forgive us!

The defeat of satan will come when Our Lord Jesus is enthroned in every heart and on the altars of the world. Some of the saints have talked about this era as the Eucharistic Reign of Jesus. Perhaps the ceaseless act of love is the precursor to that Eucharistic Reign. The ceaseless act of love will begin the reign of Jesus in each heart. The fruit of that love will be the enthronement of Jesus on every altar in the world. The Mystical Body of Christ will be united and strong, and every church will be filled with lovers of God who thirst to come and adore the Beloved of their soul and to quench His thirst to be loved. That is what the fifth vow of Children of Mary is about. We vow to give our lives, through prayer and work, that Our Eucharistic Lord will be enthroned in every heart and on every altar in the world and that all people will come to love and adore Him.

A prayer card distributed by Children of Mary.

Father, look not upon our sins but see instead
the Spotless Virgin Mary's Heart and
the Heart of Your Eucharistic Son and grant
the entire human race the grace to humbly
adore God under the appearance of bread.

O God, as once the good angels humbled themselves
to adore You appearing before them as a man,
may man humbly adore You
appearing before us as bread.

When God-with-us,
Jesus in the Holy Eucharist,
Is adored by mankind,
the head of satan will be crushed.

Imprimatur + James A. Griffin, J.D., J.C.L.
Bishop of Columbus   January 2, 2003

21

Since you are thirsting to love Me and to save souls,
Always remain in Me, never leave Me for one instant
And you will reap much fruit

Perpetual Adoration
of the Heart

We pray that, when you are able, you will go to the nearest church and adore Our Eucharistic Lord. In every Catholic Church He is in the tabernacle or on the altar in a monstrance, and He is waiting for you, longing for you to come and receive His Love and His grace, if only you come and open your heart to receive the gifts He has for you. How do you receive those gifts? By loving Him.

One of my Sisters came to me and spoke about her experience of the ceaseless act of love. She calls it, "Perpetual Adoration of the Heart." I asked her to write about it. Here is what she wrote:

"Perpetual Adoration is a great gift available in some parishes. It enables the faithful to come day or night to the feet of the living God! How wonderful it would be to never have to leave His feet, to always be there to beg His mercy upon the world: to adore, praise, thank, and console Our Lord! But we know that, no matter our state in life, duty calls us other places, and it is Jesus'

Will that we fulfill our duty. Through the continuous act of love we are enabled to remain with Our Lord constantly, to set up Perpetual Adoration of the heart! After we receive Him, let us adore and thank Him with all of our heart, mind, strength and soul for coming to us; and tell Him of our resolution to continue our adoration throughout the day by the continuous act of love.

Jesus desires to remain with us in our hearts always, even after the brief space of time that He is physically present after receiving Him Sacramentally. The Eucharistic Reign of Jesus will come about one heart at a time, and it is up to me to make Jesus Eucharistic the King of my heart. I must allow Him to reign in every area and aspect of my life, especially at those moments when my own will flares up and I begin to feel the tendency to self-rule.

When we declare Jesus Eucharistic King of our hearts, grace floods the world and many souls are drawn to do the same. If we desire to see the coming of the Eucharistic Reign of Jesus in the hearts of all men, we must be faithful to the grace given to us. When I am making an act of love, I am, in effect, saying, "I will what You Will because You are everything to me." As long as I am making the act of love, my will cannot stifle the Will of God."

Jesus told Sr. Consolata that when we are making an act of love, satan has no power over us. Please, Lord, make our lives a ceaseless act of love so that we, Your followers, will reflect Your light and love to the world and will stop adding to the darkness!

So often we Christians fail to reflect the peace, the joy, the love of God to those with whom we live, work, or do business. I see that in my life, in my own failures, on a daily basis. We are all fallen, weak creatures capable of much evil, but also, with the grace of God, capable of much good, as we see in the lives of the saints, who lived each moment in God's presence, in His love.

Surely the most basic rule of thumb for Christians to help bring the Kingdom to earth, is that we must practice the Commandments-- which, summed up, is to love God with our whole being and to love our neighbor as ourself. The essence of God, and of the Faith He took flesh to give us, is LOVE. The Holy Eucharist is the source of love that makes it possible for us to die to self and live a life of love for God and others, so It is essential. But it is also necessary to go out into the world and live that love! So when I heard about and studied the ceaseless act of love as revealed to Sr. Consolata, it was as if I found the missing piece of a puzzle—the piece that would make adoring Our Lord in the Eucharist extend throughout the day by ceaseless acts of love! That is the adoration needed that will defeat satan: ridding our lives of unnecessary words, useless thoughts--and filling our lives with ceaseless acts of love, which are spiritual Communions, and acts of love for our neighbor done solely for love of God.

22

*Yes, suffering is the most desirable thing on earth
once you understand its value,
you see that you can really prove
your love for God through it,
and finally, that it's like money with which
you can buy the salvation of souls.*

Suffering is Like Money
to Buy Souls

From time immemorial, the question has been asked of God, "If You are a God of love, why do You allow the good to suffer?" Now we hear that Jesus told Sr. Consolata that suffering is good. How can this be? Sacred Scripture tells us, that for those who love God, all things work for the good. And we know that, in order to love freely, one must freely choose to love. Free choice necessarily includes the option of refusing to love God, as did our first parents, Adam and Eve. They chose to love self over God—pride triumphed over humilty. When anyone chooses the path away from God, darkness enters the world, satan is strengthened, and suffering increases. Satan can become so strong that he induces men to become so debased that they contrive inconceivable means of inflicting pain on others. The most inhumane act in all of human history was done against God Himself—spitting in the face of God, scourging His Sacred Body, and nailing His Sacred Hands and Feet to a Cross. Those atrocities of man against God continue, as the same Jesus Who hung on the Cross and remains with us in the Holy Eucharist is being Crucified again in satanic black masses, in sacrilegious Communions, and perhaps the most grevious offense, indifference to His Presence in the Most Blessed Sacrament. Ignoring a person is one of the greatest insults, and Jesus suffers from the pain of the indifference of His followers more than He suffers from the pain inflicted by others. He suffers because He longs for our love, and love is only possible when there is a choice to love or not to love. He suffers because of those who reject His love; He suffers because of those who accept His love. Understand what I mean? Those who reject His suffering cause His suffering, but He endures that suffering because He knows that others will accept His love. So, for the sake of those who will love Him, He suffers because of those who do not.

We see how some preach a false gospel by rejecting the cross and promising health and wealth to Jesus' followers. But Catholics are Bible-believing Christians. Jesus said that, if we want to follow Him, we must pick up our cross daily. He said we must deny ourselves, put ourselves last, serve others, and associate with the lowly. He showed us by word and example that there is no greater love than to lay down one's life for another. Suppose Jesus had chosen to redeem us without suffering. We would have no example of authentic love in a world broken by sin, where all of us, in our inordinate self-love and pride, continually hurt one another—even those striving to be good. Yes, He could have redeemed us without suffering, but would there have been anyone who would have benefitted? Probably not, or at best very few. After all, to get to heaven takes more than just saying, " I accept Jesus as my Lord and Savior." Jesus tells us in Scripture, "Not everyone who says Lord, Lord will enter the Kingdom of Heaven, but only those who do the will of My Father." Being a disciple of Jesus is challenging—to die to self, love enemies, forgive everyone, deny your very self, etc., etc. Imagine if Jesus had not given us an example of all those things! Imagine a world in which people did not serve, did not forgive, did not accept suffering as part of the plan of God. Imagine the selfishness, the anger, revenge and frustration that would fill the hearts of men.

We must accept all of the Gospel, everything that Jesus commaded us to do, and not pick and choose only what we wish to accept. It is essential that each of us, who are His disciples, pick up our cross. Listen again to the words of St. Paul, "I make up in my own body what is lacking in the sufferings of Christ." Knowing that we share in the work of saving souls when we forgive and love those who hurt us and do good to all out of love for Jesus, gives purpose to our suffering. To embrace suffering for love of Christ makes us more like Christ, more capable of loving.

I remember many years ago reading a little book about total surrender to Divine Providence. It said that we should accept everything, except our own sin, as coming from the Hand of the Father. I stopped reading and asked God a question, not out of anger or disbelief, but out of a true desire to understand God's ways. I had suffered much as a little girl, and I asked Him why He would allow an innocent little child to suffer so much. I sat peacefully and silently. Then I saw in my mind's eye an image of Jesus and Mary with tears rolling down their checks. And I knew interiorly that when I was suffering, they wept. Probably as Mother Mary must have wept at the foot of the Cross. And I also knew interiorly that God allowed that suffering because through it was created in my soul a greater capacity to love. I think of it as something like a backhoe digging up out of my soul selfishness and creating more space for love of God. I didn't fully understand the mystery of iniquity, but I felt great peace and acceptance of all that had taken place in my life. In essence, to take this one incident—my childhood of suffering—it can be summed up like this. God gave free will to us all, some used that free will to do evil to me which caused suffering, and God brought good out of it. Because of that childhood suffering, I was, during most of my youth and young adulthood, a walking, open wound, looking for healing and peace and love. In my search I abandoned the Faith and, of course, found nothing but more pain; for without God there is only emptiness and sadness. But one day when a priest prayed over me, everything changed—Instant healing and, after confession, tremendous joy and knowing the love of God for me, and experiencing a great love for God and all His people. The power of the priesthood—if only they knew; if only everyone knew the power Jesus gave them to bring healing and wholeness.

Perhaps He *had to suffer* when He redeemed us, because we needed that example. What I mean is, imagine Jesus had come into the world as a King, well loved, and ascended into Heaven at the exultation of the whole world. Who would we poor sinners have to imitate? Original sin, the sin of our first parents, weakened us. Since then, it is accepting the suffering God allows to enter into our lives that strengthens us, helps us to regain, ever so slowly, the mastery of self that our first parents, before the fall, had without effort. Now we gain it "by the sweat of our brow." I remember many years ago asking Our Lord why we had to suffer. He gave me an analogy of a child injured in an accident and, afterwards needing physical therapy in order to recover the use of his legs and be able to walk again. The child would wince as he struggled to stand, then slowly take one step at a time as his legs, encumbered with braces, weighed him down. Then he would fall. Crying, he would plead with his father and mother to pick him up and help him; but they knew that, if they did so, the muscles in his legs would not grow stronger. They had to stand by with tears in their eyes and resist the urge to end his present suffering, so that someday he would have the exhilarating joy of running and playing once again.

So it is with us who are weakened with the effects of original sin. Suffering that comes from the hand of God and embraced is the therapy that will strengthen us spiritually, so that day by day we become more able to gain self-mastery over our passions and become more like God. We have a shrine at our Motherhouse called Quid Voltis. It is the scene of the crucifixion—Christ in the middle of the two thieves. In the midst of our suffering we can emulate one or the other of the two thieves. We can humbly turn to Jesus, acknowledging our sin and asking for mercy to be with Him in His Kingdom, or we can become angry, blaspheme Him, and tell Him to get us off the Cross. Quid voltis—which will you choose?

23

Does the cross I have given you please you?
It is very fruitful!
The cross of love is more fruitful
than any other cross for Me and for souls.

Purifying our Offering: Consecration to Jesus through Mary

Our Lord tells us plainly, both in words and deeds, that suffering is neccessary to save souls. We have already read about the great gift Jesus gives us when He gives us the opportunity to share in the work of salvation by offering our sufferings with His to the Father. Remember what St. Paul said, "I make up in my own body what is lacking in the sufferings of Christ for the sake of the Body, which is the Church." Our suffering is more powerful the less self-love is involved in our giving. In fact, our suffering can be absolutely worthless as far as winning any merit for ourselves, if we do not do it with love. Again St. Paul, "If I give away all I have, and if I deliver my body to be burned, but have not love, I gain nothing." (1 Cor. 13:3) Since we are striving to love God, our deeds will be done with love, but probably not purely out of selfless love. How often we hear something like, "I go help at the soup kitchen every week. It makes me feel so good!" But what if those good feelings would go away? Would she continue to serve the poor? Probably not. Our fallen human nature tends toward self-gratification and self-love. That is why God did not command us to love ourselves, but to love others as we love ourselves. Self-love is built in, even in persons who may think or say they are shy or that hate themselves; for those things are actually manifestations of pride and self-love, born of focus on self or a lack of a good thing they desire. We pray for the grace of self-forgetfulness--to serve others in good times and in bad, to love others no matter how they treat us, in other words, to love others as Jesus has loved us.

If we were determined to make our life a ceaseless act of love for selfish reasons, i.e., because we want to experience heaven on earth, our acts of love would be greatly tainted with self-love, motivated by self-interest. St. Louis de Montfort tells us that, in everything we do, there is some degree of self-love that sullies our acts of love for God and others. He spent his life promoting love for our Blessed Mother and consecrating our lives to Her, so that she could take our acts of love and clean them up, so to speak, and let her offer them to our Heavenly Father. He used this example: A small child finds an apple on the ground and wants to give it to his father. He takes it to his mother and shows it to her. She sees the wormholes and imperfections in the apple, so she takes it, cuts out the holes and bruises, slices it nicely, places it on a silver tray and presents it to the father. We can do the same when we consecrate our lives to Jesus through Mary. If that is a new concept for you, I suggest reading Fr. Michael Gaitley's book, <u>Thirty-Three Days to</u>

<u>Morning Glory</u>. He shares how consecrating his life to Mary was life changing, and provides a thirty-three day preparation for consecrating our lives to Jesus through Mary that presents devotion to Mary in a beautiful, understandable manner. And it is not too time consuming, so everyone would be able to make time for this very important act of love. Or, for the more advanced, the St. Louis de Montfort consecration is excellent. Whichever you choose, I strongly urge you to consecrate your life to Jesus through Mary. It is of tremendous importance to do so during these dramatic times in which we live. As the darkness around us thickens, Our Lady will help and guide those who have entrusted their lives to her.

24

The ceaseless act of love is more powerful
than any suffering:
so, to place myself above suffering,
I must not cease to love.

Place Myself Above Suffering?

After the Resurrection, the Ascension of Jesus, and Pentecost, the Apostles boldly preached the Gospel. The high priest had Peter and the Apostles arrested and put in prison, from which they were miraculously freed by an angel. The next day, "After recalling the apostles, they had them flogged, ordered them to stop speaking in the name of Jesus, and dismissed them. So they left the presence of the Sanhedrin, rejoicing that they had been found worthy to suffer dishonor for the sake of the name." (Acts 5: 40-41)

The Lord allows us to suffer, but always with the grace to endure. He knows what is best for each soul, for each situation. To suffer with love expands our capacity to love, and so grow in likeness to Jesus Our Lord. We beg grace to embrace with love any cross He wishes us to carry. Embracing with love Jesus our Lord along with the cross He has placed on our shoulders does indeed make the yoke sweet—sweet because of the good that will come with the gift of our cross.

25

If a creature of good will desires to love Me
and to make of her life one single act of love
from the moment of her rising until she falls asleep
at night—from the heart, be it well understood—
then I will perform incredible things for that soul.
Write that down!

Summary

Jesus is asking for one ceaseless act of love from the moment of rising until falling asleep at night-- "Jesus, Mary, I love You. Save souls."--unless duty or charity require otherwise. And when duty and charity do require otherwise, our act of love will continue by doing our duty and acts of charity out of love for Him. The foundation of this ceaseless act of love is, first of all, to love Jesus and, for love of Him, to love His Church—the One, Holy, Catholic and Apostolic Church that He founded and through which He remains with us in order to distribute the graces He won for us on Calvary. He distributes those graces to us principally through the Holy Eucharist. So we love Jesus in the Holy Eucharist; we adore Him and receive Him as often as we possibly can. We rid our lives of attachment to things, useless thoughts and unnecessary words, and strive to fill our minds and hearts only with love for Him, reciting the act of love continuously even, if possible, while going about our duties and performing acts of charity.

We make our lives a ceaseless act of love through these means:

1. A Communion of Love. The Eucharist is Jesus, Who stays with us in the Holy Eucharist and is longing for an exchange of love. Center your life around the Mass, attending Mass, everyday if possible, and receiving Holy Communion with love. Jesus is the source of Love. Receiving Him in Holy Communion with love will sustain you in the ceaseless act of love.

2. Desire and Adoration, when it is a movement of the heart that longs for Him, a longing to receive Him in Holy Communion when not able to do so, is a spiritual communion, an act of love. Likewise, adoring Our Eucharistic Lord is an essential part of a ceaseless act of love.

3. Words of love, either silent and interior or vocal, i.e., "Jesus, Mary, I love You. Save souls." (Jesus said this is His favorite formula for an act of love. Other prayers said from the heart are acts of love as well.)

4. Acts of charity, when done *solely for love of Jesus and with a sweet smile!*

5. Doing our duty, even if that means concentrating on our work and not being able to make the act of love in words.

6. Suffering willingly is saying "yes" to God, proves our love for Him, and gives us an opportunity to share in the work of saving souls when we accept our cross for love of God.

To make our life a ceaseless act of love is a process that requires patience, spending our lifetime *trying* to control our thoughts, refraining from uttering unnecessary words, and detaching our hearts from things of this world. Don't get discouraged, and don't give up! Pray for perseverance, and ask your guardian angel to help you remember to make acts of love upon rising in the morning till you fall asleep at night. It is well worth it!

Union with God--and the peace and joy that is the fruit of that union--comes to the degree that we are purified of self-seeking and are filled with Divine Love. It is Love that purifies and perfects. The ceaseless act of love is a concrete way to begin the process of purification and perfection now, and deepen our union with God. At death, for souls in the state of grace, any stain of sin will be cleansed in purgatory. How are souls in purgatory cleansed? Last night I read A Treatise on Purgatory by St. Catherine of Genoa. In it she explains how our transformation into Love is brought about by Love!

Here is part of that treatise:

> "I behold such a great conformity between God and the soul, that when He finds her pure as when His Divine Majesty first created her He gives her an attractive force of ardent love which would annihilate her if she were not immortal. He so transforms her into Himself that, forgetting all, she no

longer sees aught beside Him; and He continues to draw her toward Him, inflames her with love, and never leaves her until He has brought her to that state from whence she first came forth, that is, to the perfect purity in which she was created.

"When the soul beholds within herself the amorous flame by which she is drawn toward her sweet Master and her God, the burning heat of love overpowers her and she melts. Then, in that divine light she sees how God, by His great care and constant providence, never ceases to attract her to her last perfection, and that He does so through pure love alone. She sees, too, that she herself, clogged by sin, cannot follow that attraction toward God, that is, that reconciling glace which He casts upon her that He may draw her to Himself. Moreover, a comprehension of that great misery, which it is to be hindered from gazing upon the light of God, is added to the instinctive desire of the soul to be wholly free to yield herself to that unifying flame. I repeat, it is the view of all these things which causes the pain of the suffering souls in Purgatory, not that they esteem their pains as great (cruel though they be), but they count as far worse that opposition which they find in themselves to the will of that God whom they behold burning for them with so ardent and so pure a love.

"This love, with its unifying regard is ever

drawing these souls, as if it had no other thing to do; and when the soul beholds this, if she could find a yet more painful purgatory in which she could be more quickly cleansed, she would plunge at once therein, compelled by the burning, mutual love between herself and God.'"

We were created by Love for Love—for God alone. The only marriage in Heaven will be the marriage of each soul with God--where we will partake of the Wedding Feast of the Lamb for all eternity in unimaginable bliss of Love and joy and peace! Ask Our Lady for the grace to persevere, to never give up in striving to make your life a ceaseless act of love. What better way to spend one's life!

26

Prepare the world for the coming of my love.

A Call to Holiness

The Lord is offering us a gift for these times. Come, my friends, all you who love Jesus and want to love Him all the time--with all your heart, all your mind, all your strength and all your soul. This is something none of us can do on our own, but God is eager to give us the grace if our desire and generosity are sufficient. Let us pray for one another--all who undertake this mysterious journey deep into the Heart of God!

St. Faustina November 27, 1936

"Today, I was in heaven in spirit, and I saw its unconceivable beauties and the happiness that awaits us after death. I saw how great is happiness in God, which spreads to all creatures, making them happy; and then all the glory and praise which springs from this happiness returns to its source; and they enter into the depths of God contemplating the inner life of God the Father, the Son, and the Holy Spirit, whom they will never comprehend or fathom. This source of happiness is unchanging in its essence, but it is always new, gushing forth happiness for all creatures. Now I understand Saint Paul, who said, "Eye has not seen, nor has ear heard, not has it entered into the heart of man what God has prepared for those who love him." And God has given me to understand that there is but one thing that is of infinite value in His eyes, **and that is love of God; love, love and once again, love; and <u>nothing can compare with a single act of pure love of God</u>**. Oh, with what inconceivable favors God gifts a soul that loves Him sincerely! **Oh, how happy is the soul who already here on earth enjoys His special favors! And of such are the little and humble souls.**

Let's satiate Jesus' thirst to be loved! Not because it will mean more glory for ourselves or for any other reason, but purely out of love for God alone! Let's attend daily Mass and, from one Holy Communion to the next, make acts of love. Doing so will transform our lives and bring much grace to the world. As our union with God deepens, the grace we receive will increase. Suarez teaches that "when sanctifying grace is in operation with all of its inner activity, it becomes doubled; thus, if a just person does an action, whatever it is, as perfectly as possible and out of pure love for God, whatever grace was already in him is doubled through this action.." (Suarez in 3p. tom.II dis. 18) Scripture tells us that the prayers of a just man are powerful indeed. Receiving Jesus with love in Holy Communion, going to adoration, and practicing the continuous act of love will make our prayers powerful, and much grace will go out into the whole world. The terrible darkness will decrease, and the light of Love will grow stronger and stronger. This light will be the grace that will free innumerable souls from satan's grasp.

*Yes, the hearts of the Littlest Souls are destined
to die of love for Me,
to be consumed exclusively for Me.*

"Yes, the Littlest Souls are the pupil of my eyes."

(Jesus to Sr. Consolata)

To order more books visit: www.childrenofmary.net
email: childrenofmarysisters@gmail.com
OR call: (513) 713-0432

PART II

The Littlest Way of Love

**Abridged message
from the Heart of Jesus
to Venerable Sister
Consolata Betrone**

By
Fr. Lorenzo Sales, IMC

Table of contents

Foreword

A Way and a Mission

Sr. Consolata Betrone, a Capuchin nun, (1903-1946) had the mission of contributing to the spiritual renewal of the world by showing souls the "Littlest Way of Love.[1]" This way can be summarized into three points:

1. Making an internal, ceaseless act of love.
2. Say a cheerful "yes" to everyone, since it's Jesus we see and deal with in everyone.
3. Say a grateful "Yes" to everything God asks of us.

The premise of this new way is a ceaseless love that unites the soul to Christ. This is how one more readily loves one's neighbor out of love for the Lord, and eagerly accepts all sacrifices.

Jesus Himself taught Sr. Consolata the words of the act of love which would be most agreeable to Him: "Jesus, Mary, I love You. Save souls!" He insistently requested that she repeat this prayer, if only in her mind, as often as she was allowed to by her duties.

---

[1] *Jesus Appeals to the World*, Alba House, 200 p. 1957, 2187 Victory Blvd, Staten Island, N.Y. 10314, U.S.A.

This booklet is a faithful summary of the writings of Sr. Consolata Betrone found in: "Jesus Appeals to the World" and in the "Biographie de Soeur Consolata Betrone.[2]"

We are therefore grateful to these works. We are happy to condense certain passages here, and to bring to light those which specifically deal with the "Littlest Way of Love" which was revealed to the modest religious capuchin by Our Lord.

We have chosen a catechism style of question and answer because this seemed to be the best way to achieve our end, which was making each point we touched upon easily understandable by the reader.

We eagerly recommend this booklet to all little souls for their own spiritual benefit, and for a greater and more widespread knowledge of the doctrine it contains.

Fr. L. Sales

---

[2] *Biographie de Socur Consolata Betrone*, by L. Sales, M.C., Editions Salvator, 486 p., 1953.

Love and Acts of Love

1. What is so special about the act of love?

1. The act of love is part of the supreme perfection of the theological virtue of Charity, the queen of all virtues. It brings them to birth, sustains them, gives them life and perfects them[3]. Faith and Hope are Charity's sisters; but they halt on the threshold of eternity. Because Faith will be replaced with Vision, and Hope with possession, only love enters heaven and remains there eternally[4].

2. The act of love is also the most sanctifying, because it unites us to God, Who is infinite holiness[5], in the most direct and intimate way.

3. For the same reasons, the act of love is the most apostolically fruitful in that which pertains to the salvation of souls[6].

---

[3] "In the same way as the branches of a tree are all attached to the same trunk, so do all the virtues proceed from love." (St. Gregory The Great, Hom. 27, in Eveng. Vig. Apost.)

[4] "Love will have no end...Now only those three things remain: Faith, Hope, and Charity, but the greatest of all is Love." (1 Cor. 13:8-13).

[5] "If anyone loves Me, He will keep My commandments, and My Father will love him, and We will come to him and We will make Our home in him" (John 14:23), "God is love, and whoever lives in love, lives in God, and God in him" (1 John 4:16).

3

2. What is the value of the act of perfect charity according to the doctrine of the Church?

1. An act of perfect love for God immediately reconciles the soul with God, even if it's full of mortal sins, and even before sacramental confession, as long as the will to confess is present[7].

2. Even more importantly, an act of perfect love purifies us of venial sins[8].

3. After a serious sin, an act of perfect love (accompanied by the intention to go to confession) can immediately return to us the merits we lost, along with sanctifying grace. It can even enable us to acquire more merits, something that would have been impossible for us even through good works, as long as we were still in a state of sin.

---

[6] "He who remains in Me and I in him will bear much fruit" (John 15:5). That is, fruits of sanctity and of saving souls. "The tiniest act of pure love has more value in God's eyes, and is more useful to the Church and to the soul itself, than all other exterior works as a whole." (St. John of the Cross, Cant. spir., str. 27.) "A single act of love is more glorious than all the apostolates in the universe." (B.J. Eymard, Euch. League of Milan, 1925.)

[7] Council of Trent, Sess. 14, c.4.

[8] "Love covers a multitude of sins" (1 Peter 4:18).

4. An act of perfect love, like every other supernatural action, diminishes the sorrows of purgatory; it can obtain a complete remission for us if it's accomplished with a zeal and perfection whose value only God can appreciate[9].

5. Every act of perfect love further develops the state of unity between God and the soul, and consequently also the divine life within the soul[10].

6. Every act of perfect love, like every other supernatural action, earns us an increase in sanctifying grace, which, in its turn, increasingly affects our actions. In addition to that, it earns us a greater glory in heaven.

3. What is perfect love?

1. Perfect love is loving God for Himself, and finding our happiness in Him.

2. This level of perfection in love is preceded by two others. These are: initial love, and progressive love. Initial love consists mostly of the flight from sin, and of resistance to its

---

[9] Cf. Saint Thomas, Supp. Q. 5 a. 2,3,
[10] "He who unites himself with the Lord is one with Him in spirit." (1 Cor. 6:17) And love is precisely what unites us to God, as St. Thomas explains: "Love causes man to offer himself to God, remaining with Him in a real spiritual union.

lures; it finds impetus in motives stemming from the holy fear of God. Progressive love works to acquire virtue, and when discouraged, is sustained by the hope of a reward.

3. In these normal progressions of love, all the motives dovetail harmoniously, and while acquiring divine benefits, the soul finally opens to that perfect love through which God is loved for Himself.

4. This pure and perfect love produces virtues, and strives to procure glory for God.

4. Is it possible to make acts of perfect Love?

1. Acts of perfect love are not only possible, but become easy. This is how: since these actions are, shall we say, the result of repeated efforts by the soul to arrive at friendship love with God, once the soul reaches a certain degree of love intensity, it experiences the need to find release in flights of blazing love, which seem to assuage its oppressed heart...

2. When I say "Jesus, I love You," and reaffirm the total gift of myself to Him through the difficulties I encounter and the fatigue I experience, and I do it because He is worthy of being loved, honored, and faithfully served, I make an act of perfect love. The act of charity which we learn in the catechism is a perfect act of love.

3. Even in the initial and progressive levels, a perfect act of love already facilitates the flight from sin and the exercise of virtue, because it continually demands and brings about an intimate experience of the supreme motive of love, which is the infinite goodness of God.

5. Can we make an act of perfect love on our own?

Whether making an act of perfect love, or doing any other supernatural action, it's always necessary to be helped by grace. God never refuses to help anyone who wants to love Him. Let's not forget that He Himself made love a commandment, and requires it from all men.

6. Does the element of "feelings" enter into the perfection of the act of love?

"Feelings" are not at all necessary in an act of perfect love. I can love God with a perfect and intense love, even with an icy heart, even while experiencing disgust or aversion. To love God with an act of perfect love, it's enough to want to love Him in that way. In these circumstances, the act of love can be even purer, more generous, and therefore more meritorious and agreeable to God.

7. *In how many ways can we make acts of perfect love?*

1. As far as God is concerned, we can make acts of perfect love of all of our actions, even the most minor ones, even those which are indifferent in themselves (eating, drinking, sleeping)[11].

2. Also, offering the sacrifices inherent to our daily duties, our daily sufferings whether little or large, to God with love.

3. By multiplying our acts of perfect love throughout the day. It doesn't matter if they are simple internal or external acts (like an invocation,) as long as they always spring from internal love.

8. *Is multiplying acts of perfect love a useful thing to do?*

It's a very holy and useful thing for the soul to do.

1. To obey the first commandment in all of its perfection;

2. To exercise, develop and perfect the theological virtue of Charity within ourselves, in

---

[11] "So whether you eat or whether you drink, or whatever you do, do it all for the glory of God." (1 Cor. 10:31)

order to develop and perfect all of the other virtues along with it;

3. Because it's a big help for the soul to put its purity of intention into all of its actions;

4. To augment the supernatural value of our actions, by increasing sanctifying grace within ourselves[12];

5. To increase the fervor of our religious devotions, and even substitute for them when it is impossible for us to accomplish them;

6. To help us give the maximum value to every instant of our short earthy journey for the glory of God, our own sanctification, and the salvation of souls.

7. Because it will be easier for us to make our death a holocaust of love, if we've made our life a sacrifice of love.

---

[12] Suarez teaches that, "when sanctifying grace is in operation with all of its inner activity, it becomes doubled: thus if a just person does an action, whatever it is, as perfectly as possible, and out of pure love for God, whatever grace was already in him is doubled, through this action." (Suarez, in 3 p. tom. II, disp. 18.) Love increases grace and grace augments love. The more one loves, the more capable of loving one becomes.

9. Wouldn't it be sufficient to state our intention at the beginning of each day?

It would be sufficient, at most, for giving our actions throughout the day a supernatural value, but not for obtaining this fullness of supernatural or divine life that Jesus earned for us, and which He would like to see in us[13]. In other words, and to better develop this idea:

1. The intention stated at the beginning of the day can easily be displaced by other less perfect intentions. By making frequent acts of perfect love, we place ourselves beyond the reach of this danger.

2. Real love is more perfect than love that is simply given out of habit, so it affects our spiritual life even more completely.

3. By making frequent acts of perfect love we nourish and perfect our internal life—the real life of the soul—in the best way thus avoiding the dissipation of the spirit which would deprive us of precious time for all eternity.

4. Loving God with a real love, in whatever measure is possible to each individual is a

---

[13] Saint Thomas teaches that charity is perfect "when one loves as much as one is able." This precept of love has no limits. It asks us to always continue to grow in love. God, Who is the Infinite Good, deserves to be loved without measure.

part of, as we have already said and as we will see more clearly later, this perfect love with which God wants us to love Him, and which He has ordained from us in the first commandment.

5. The fact of multiplying acts of love helps the soul to accomplish another divine precept: "One should always pray, and not give up." (Luke 18:1) St. Paul often brings it up: "Pray ceaselessly." (1 Thessalonians 5:17) The act of love is not only the very best of prayers, but even as short, easy and completely internal as it is, it makes the adherence to this commandment admirably simple, without overly tiring the spirit with multiple and complex formulas.

10. Does what we've just said apply to all Christians?

1. Yes, because all Christians are required to aim for perfect love by the first commandment.

2. We would also like to say that the practice of the act of love, in certain regards, is more suited to people living in the world and active religious than to those who are living in cloisters. The latter are, in effect, drawn by their surroundings and their lives of prayer to a constant union with God; while it's far more difficult for active religious, and even more for people living in the world,

because of the variety and nature of their daily occupations, as well as their many material preoccupations. And besides, they also aren't in a position to make long vocal prayers.

3. In contrast, an act of love is quickly made! It doesn't take effort, and doesn't interrupt external activity; on the contrary, it gives life and sanctifies the activity for eternity. In this way, the soul takes on the habit of making acts of love little by little. It becomes more and more intimately united to God, even to becoming, with time, virtually ceaseless.

4. This explains why the doctrine pertaining to the ceaseless act of love, as given to Sr. Consolata Betrone by Jesus, and outlined in the book "Jesus Speaks to the World", has drawn as much interest from people living in the world as from souls consecrated to God.

A Few Thoughts

(Excerpts from the lessons given to Sr. Consolata by Jesus)

Consolata, tell the world how good and maternal I am, and how I only ask for love in exchange. Today, like yesterday, like tomorrow, I ask for nothing but love of My poor creatures. Oh! If you could descend into each heart and pour torrents of the caresses of My love into them! I burn with the desire to be lovingly served by My creatures. It's not the avoidance of sin out of fear for My punishments that I desire. I want to be loved. I want the love of My creatures; and once they love Me, they won't offend Me any longer.

Love Me, Consolata. Love only Me. There is everything in love. When you love Me, you give Jesus everything He desires from His creatures: love.

Only divine love can transform apostates into apostles; dirtied lilies into immaculate lilies; sinners covered in vices into trophies of mercy.

Put all of your attention into doing your daily duty, so that you can make it with all possible love. Your actions will be so much more valuable, and you will grow even more quickly in love.

Transform any disagreeable thing you meet in your daily walk into bouquets of flowers. Gather them with love, and offer them to Me with love. Gifts? This is how I appreciate them: when they are given with all possible love. This is how even your most insignificant actions become precious.

Consolata, tell souls that I prefer an act of love and a Communion of love over any other gift they could offer Me.

Yes, I prefer an act of love over a discipline, because I am thirsty for love.

Consolata, write this down—I am demanding this obedience from you—that for a single one of your acts of love, I would create Paradise.

Love Me, Consolata. Love will make all shortcomings disappear.

Love is holiness. The more you love Me, the holier you will become. Remember that it is love, and love alone, that will carry you, victorious, to every summit.

Love Me and you will be happy; and the more you love Me, the happier you will be. Oh, if people loved Me, what joy would reign in this most miserable world!

Formula for a Ceaseless Act of Love

11. *What is the formula for making a ceaseless act of love?*

The formula for making a ceaseless act of love, as dictated to Sister Consolata Betrone by Jesus, is as follows: *Jesus, Mary, I love You. Save souls!*

12. *Why a formula?*

Because, it's part of our nature to condense and express, through the use of formulas, the sentiments of our soul. We find a confirmation of that in all of the liturgies of the Church, and in the consent it gives to so many prayers and invocations. As for the rest, isn't it in the Holy Scriptures that the saints in heaven (Apocalypse 4:6) and the angels (Isaiah 6:3) express their ardent love by endlessly repeating "Holy, holy, holy is the Lord, God of hosts"?

13. *What is the intrinsic value of this formula?*

1. It expresses an act of perfect and pure love (as has previously been explained).

2. It unites the love of the most Holy Virgin Mary to the love of Jesus (and through Him to God, the Holy Trinity).

3. It unites the love of God to the love of neighbor, by making entreaties in favor of all souls. It contains not only an act of perfect love, but also one of perfect charity. And the entire Law is summed up in love and charity.

14. What is the extrinsic value of this formula?

Its extrinsic value resides in this: it comes directly from Jesus, who conferred an anointing and a particular value upon it, summarized in the promises He made to Sister Consolata Betrone.

15. Can't the uniformity of the formula seem monotonous?

All souls are free to follow the spirit's leads to advance in perfection in Love; it would therefore seem that:

a) it's less tiring for the spirit to utilize a single formula rather than many different ones;

b) it's a help for the soul, since it will make it easier for the act of love to become a habit;

c) in any case, the monotony doesn't hinder the perfection of love, or the value of the act of love, in any way. Rather, it renders it more meritorious, because of the greater effort necessary to remain attentive. Of course, the repetition of the recited prayers during the Rosary can hinder certain spiritual conditions, but that

16

doesn't stop the holy Rosary from being well recommended!

16. What can be said about the formula relative to exercising a ceaseless act of love?

1. The formula serves to set the spirit, the will and the heart on the perfection of love, and upon the object of that love: Jesus, Mary, souls. The goal: a life of love, intimacy with Jesus. The means: is the ceaseless act of love, and the formula is a help for practicing this act.

2. Since it's an act of love, it's not necessary to pronounce the formula out loud. The act of love is an internal action of the will which wants to love, of the heart which does love. It's evident that, in certain moments of struggle or dryness, the vocal recitation of the formula can be a help for the soul.

3. It's therefore unnecessary to believe that making a ceaseless act of love, even when set in a formula, is made better by the mechanical repetition of this formula. A ceaseless act of love, even set in this way, must above all else be a continuous, silent and ardent effusion of love and charity.

4. Insofar as what Jesus wants from us, it's not the number of acts of love that is most important. Between two people, if the former makes a thousand successive acts of

love, or nearly that many, and the latter makes a lesser number, but slips them into every free moment of the day, and remains closely united to Jesus, then it's the latter person who will have better understood the Little Way of Love.

17. ***What can be said about the formula of a ceaseless act of love relative to indulgenced invocations?***

1. The formula "Jesus, Mary, I love You. Save souls!" has an indulgence attached to it (300 days, granted by Cardinal Fossati, the archbishop of Turin). It can therefore be used by everyone as an invocation to obtain the attached indulgence.

2. Meanwhile, let's not forget that the internal act of perfect love is, itself, the Indulgence of indulgences, as Jesus explained to Sr. Consolata, and as we have seen, according to the doctrine of the Church on the value of an act of love.

It remains understood that this act, this prayer, must always be made with a will for perfection.

A Few Thoughts

**(Excepts from the lessons given to
Sr. Consolata by Jesus)**

Consolata, establish within yourself a continuous "Jesus, Mary, I love You. Save souls!" Consider that it's the only resolution that will allow you to answer "YES" to all of My requests for sacrifices.

Why don't I permit you many oral prayers? Because the act of love is more fertile. A single "Jesus, Mary, I love You. Save souls!" makes up for a thousand blasphemies. Tell Me, what prayer can anyone say to Me that is more beautiful? "Jesus, Mary, I love You. Save souls!": Love and souls, what could anyone want that would be more beautiful?

Consolata, I promise that I will make you reach all the summits of Love, and of sorrow. You, just live and say "Jesus, Mary, I love You. Save souls!" Nothing else.

Remember that an act of love on your part can decide the salvation of a soul, its eternal salvation. So see that you don't waste a single "Jesus, Mary, I love You. Save souls!"

"Jesus, Mary, I love You. Save souls!" includes everything: the souls in purgatory, as well as those in the militant Church; the innocent soul, as well as the guilty one, the dying one, the atheist, etc., all souls.

A ceaseless act of love contains all resolutions: by practicing it, you accomplish everything else.

Live, annihilated and enclosed in a single perpetual "Jesus, Mary, I love You. Save souls!" Nothing, no one, must exist for you, except for the act of love.

Follow Me in a ceaseless act of love, day by day, hour by hour, minute by minute; I Myself will take care of all the rest, I Myself will provide.

Do you know what your cross is? To not miss a single act of love. I love you, and this cross which I place on your shoulders annihilates everything within you; at the same time it permits you to scrupulously observe all of the points of the Rule, the Constitutions, the Directory.

As long as you remain in Me by a continuing act of love, you live a marvelous and divine Life.

If a creature of good will loves Me and wants to make his life an act of love (with the heart, as understood) from awakening until the moment of sleep, I will do enormous things for this soul. Write it down.

Continuity in the Act of Love

18. How is the continuity in the act of love to be understood?

1. According to the lessons Jesus gave Sr. Consolata, continuity in the act of love should be understood in this way: when praying or meditating, when working out of duty, charity or necessity; when, through obligation, we are busy with occupations that absorb our internal faculties, the act of love is perpetuated by intention. Jesus counts it as well, even if the spirit and the heart aren't able to concentrate seriously on love in those moments.

2. It's therefore unnecessary to sacrifice duty for love (which would be a contradiction) but rather to sanctify duty with love.

3. Moreover, it gives an eternal value to the numerous moments of the day which, quite often through lack of vigilance or self-control, risk being lost in daydreams or useless indiscretions.

4. Every instant of our earthly life is a gift from God, and contains within itself an inestimable eternal value. Why willingly waste a single one? The act of love is a great help for imbuing each instant of our free time with such value.

19. Is continuity possible with the act of love?

1. There is an effective and absolute continuity: loving God with a real love from the moment of awakening in the morning until going to sleep at night, without loosing sight of the presence of God for even one short instant, and loving Him ceaselessly with a real love, even through our most absorbing or distracting occupations. That kind of continuity isn't possible for human nature without being specially privileged by God. The Holy Virgin was indisputably privileged in this way. While on earth, She loved God with a perfection superior to the very Seraphim of heaven.

2. There is a continuity which is moral and effective: to not willingly waste a single act of love during those moments when the heart and spirit are free to love. Even that continuity is impossible on this earth without a special grace from God. And God isn't obliged to give it to anyone. However, He can bless a few souls with it, at least for a while.

3. Finally, there is the moral continuity of love, which is not an effective one, but one of will and effort: to push oneself to not voluntarily waste a single act of love, even when the effort is unsuccessful, by making a renewed effort after failures of greater or lesser duration, caused by absentmindedness or

instability. This continuity is always possible with the help of God for every soul of good will, and it's precisely this continuity of love that Jesus asks of humble souls.

20. Understood in this way, is continuity of love part of the perfection of love which the first commandment asks of us?

1. God doesn't demand the impossible, but perfection: His law can only be one of perfection. Therefore, if He requires us to love with all our heart, it's because we are capable of doing so, and we must drive ourselves to love Him in that way. If He commands us to love Him with our entire spirit, our entire soul and all of our strength, it's because we are capable of doing so, and we must do so.

2. That's why the effort the soul makes to keep itself as closely united to God as is possible for the heart and spirit is a part of the aforementioned perfection of love, and is an actual duty, even if the means of obtaining this end are not the same for all souls.

3. The means that Jesus proposed to Sr. Consolata is the act of love. So, when Jesus asked Sr. Consolata to push herself to make her life into a ceaseless act of virginal love, He only asked her to put into practice that which is inherently contained in the first commandment.

4. The means for attaining this continuity of love can vary from soul to soul, therefore souls are called to different degrees of perfection in the continuity of love. The important thing is for each soul to dedicate all of its strength to achieving this perfection.

21. What kind of continuity of love did Sr. Consolata have?

1. During the first years, after Jesus asked her to give Him a ceaseless act of love, it was a continuity of will and effort. Progress was slow, and consisted mostly of the elimination of all voluntary lapses in the exercise of love. During the last two years, Jesus gave her the grace of a moral and effective continuity. That is the one which consists of not voluntarily losing a single opportunity to make an act of love between one Communion and the next.

2. This is in regards to Sr. Consolata's active part in the exercise of a ceaseless act of love. It is evident that Jesus also gave her the free gift of being able to consider her entire life as having been a ceaseless act of love.

22. What can be said about the vow of ceaseless love?

1. By making this vow, the soul takes on the obligation of never voluntarily wasting an act of love from one Communion to the next.

2. Since this is one of the most arduous vows, it must be considered very, very carefully before pronouncing it, or allowing other souls to undertake it. It should only be permitted for souls which have a deep internal life, for souls which have already practiced ceaseless acts of love for a long time, in all spiritual conditions and have practically arrived at a continuity of moral love through will and effort.

3. In any case, it would be better if the soul did not bind itself suddenly and perpetually, but rather advance in this way in successive stages; and never on pain of sinning, but rather of simple imperfection.

A Few Thoughts

**(Excerpts from the lessons given to
Sr. Consolata by Jesus)**

I am asking a ceaseless "Jesus, Mary, I love You. Save souls!" from you, from the moment you rise in the morning until you go to bed at night. If you think I'm omnipotent, then believe that I can give you this continual act of love; I want it.

Love Me continually. It doesn't matter if your heart is made of stone or ice!

Everything is contained in, everything is dependent on a continual act of love.

Say goodbye forever to all that is created and to this world, and escape into a ceaseless act of love. You see, each has his own tastes. Here are mine: smallness, nothingness, annihilation, but love.

It doesn't matter if the demon, if your passions, set loose every possible tempest within your soul. Thunder, wind, lightning will be impotent against you. You must tell yourself, "I want to continue, dauntlessly, my act of love from one Communion to the next; that is my duty, my only duty." And go forward!

The ceaseless act of love is your standard; defend it before the enemy (even at the cost of your life).

All that tempts you to turn away from a ceaseless act of love would not come from Me, but from the enemy.

Love Me always, through the battle and the inevitable falls; train yourself to remain unimpressed by failure, but to continue, impervious, your act of love.

You do the impossible to give Me a ceaseless act of love, but when you fail, I Myself will make reparation. No, don't be afraid, I will not stop being good.

Don't you think I can give you this ceaseless act of love? You see, it pleases Me to see you struggle, fall, get up, to see your strengths at work, to see what you know how to do. Shall I tell you what pleases Me the most? It's to see you firm, rising above everything, seeing you continue your act of love.

For your faithfulness to the ceaseless act of love to become heroic, it's necessary to will it, strongly will it, heroically will it.

The Virginity of the Ceaseless Act of Love

23. What does "virginity of love" mean?

You practice virginity of love by maintaining a spirit which is free of all that could prevent it from concentrating on God, in order to love Him.

24. What are the virginity of love's specifics?

Specifically, it is a threefold virginity of spirit, of the tongue, and of the heart.

25. How is virginity of the spirit practiced?

It is practiced by the effort made by the soul which does not want to voluntarily allow even the tiniest useless thought.

26. And what are these useless thoughts?

1. Mostly, they concern the past (we can't go back there), or the future (which is out of our hands), and so far as the present moment, all thoughts which do not pertain to the duty at hand, and to which it's necessary to apply our spirit.

2. Preoccupations of all sorts, voluntarily engaged in, or prolonged beyond necessity[14].

3. The soul centering in on itself, which is quite easily begun and nurtured, and therefore detrimental to its spiritual good.

27. What is meant by the "soul centering in on itself"?

1. For example if, within the spirit, a soul unnecessarily dwells on a more or less voluntary lapse, the soul not only does not get anything out of it, it wastes its time. But the soul can also be upset, even discouraged, when it goes so far as to listen to the insinuations of self-love. Conversely—if after having asked forgiveness from God, renewed its good intentions and made reparation for infidelity—the soul no longer dwells on it, but continuing the song of love makes an even greater work, and stops wasting time, that's when it will advance.

2. Other situations which are useless and dangerous to dwell on are reprimands, humiliations, and failure in endeavors. It's better to abandon them to God, no longer think about them, and continue to love.

---

[14] "Seek first the Kingdom of God and His righteousness, and all of these things shall be added unto you. Do not worry about tomorrow, for tomorrow will worry about itself." (Matt. 6: 33-34)

3. Or yet again, when the soul gets lost in suppositions and conjectures concerning things that have been said or left unsaid, done or left undone, on the why of this or that disposition regarding it. Those are all times that the devil steals from the soul, and which would have been more usefully employed in loving.

28. How is virginity of the tongue practiced?

It's practiced by being vigilant over oneself to avoid all useless speech, and any talking not required by duty, charity, or necessity[15].

29. How is virginity of the heart practiced?

1. It's practiced by fighting against inquisitiveness, either about the events of the world (curiosity, etc.,) or about one's neighbor (being interested in another's private life).

2. It's also practiced, by those souls which are already advanced in the perfection of love, by refusing the heart all human satisfaction, even those that are not bad. God alone, in the spirit and the heart. He alone is sufficient for everything.

30. What is the objective of this threefold virginity?

---

[15] "I tell you that men will have to give an account on the day of judgment for every idle word they have spoken." (Matt. 12:36)

1. It's always the same: raising the soul to the perfection of love. Thoughts, curiosities, useless words which are voluntarily said are imperfections of love, failures in the perfect life of love. If Jesus condemns all useless words in the Gospel, it's because they are a fault for the soul and they steal precious moments that could have been consecrated to loving God.

2. On the other hand, if we don't make silence (internal and external) a means for reaching the perfection of love, then the silence is senseless. It is then no longer virtuous and could therefore simply become an affected and useless muteness.

31. Is the virginity of love possible for the soul?

We will repeat what we've already said about the continuity of the act of love: what counts the most before God is good will and the soul's constant and generous effort. The rest, that is the success, doesn't depend on the soul but on the divine grace which God, in His loving designs on the soul, bestows on it. We won't be judged on our successes, but rather on the effort we made to succeed. Useless thoughts, words, superfluous curiosities, which the soul does not want, against which it fights, don't impede the perfection of love but make it more meritorious before God.

32. What is the relationship between virginity of love and the ceaseless act of love?

They are both reciprocal. The virginity of love (or the battle against useless thoughts and words) is necessary for exercising a ceaseless act of love. Of its own, the exercise of a ceaseless act of love is a very efficient means to achieve the aforementioned threefold virginity; it helps the soul to set its spirit and heart on God.

33. Is there a difference between the virginity of love and the virginity of the act of love?

They are substantially the same. Still, Jesus asks Sr. Consolata expressly for "the virginity of a ceaseless act of love;" the endless gift, virginally pure, without an admixture of other thoughts, however good.

34. Why exclude thoughts "however good"?

1. If for example, I pondered on my future, I could certainly do it in a good way and therefore the thought would be good; but if I confide it all to Jesus, Who thinks of everything to the last detail, and I consecrate the present moment to thinking about Him and loving Him, I then accomplish a far more perfect thing.

2. Here is the other reason Jesus gave Sr. Consolata: "The good thoughts which penetrate your heart can carry within themselves self-love, complacency and can

threaten the integrity of the act of love. But, if while trusting blindly in Me, you have confidence that I will provide in all ways, not letting any thought penetrate into you, then your act of love will have a virginal purity." As can be seen, there are nuances of perfection. Only the souls which have attained a high degree in the life of love can perceive them.

35. Of what does the vow of virginal love consist?

The vow of virginal love, requested of Sr. Consolata by Jesus, consists in undertaking the prevention of any voluntary thought, word, or useless attachment, with the aim of loving in a virginal and ceaseless way.

36. What can be said about this vow?

All that we have said about the vow of ceaseless love.

A Few Thoughts

(Excerpts from the lessons given to Sr. Consolata by Jesus)

Consolata, you know how much I love you! You see, even if My heart is divine, it's also human like yours. It thirsts for your love, for all your thoughts and wants them all.

I will think of everything, even the tiniest things; you, think only of Me, I'm thirsty for your love. All of it. Don't add a single stray thought, it would be a thorn in My head.

Give Me all of your words, I want them all. I want your continual silence. I want you to be all Mine.

Always observe silence; be miserly with words, even the necessary ones; answer everyone with smiles and always wear a pleasant countenance.

Forget everything completely, think only of loving Me more and more; concentrate all of your thoughts, your heart-beats, the silence, on this alone: loving.

Say goodbye forever to every thought, to every word. Let others do whatever they want; you, be in Me, and you will bear much fruit, because I will be the One acting in you.

Put all of your efforts into being firmly united to the "Life," into not becoming detached from "Jesus only," into having no other thought (I think of everything), into not saying a single word that isn't required of you.

The thoughts that come to you, Consolata, and which you don't want, are not acts of infidelity.

I am leaving you the struggle against useless thoughts because it's meritorious for you. When we decide to do nothing but love, all obstacles to love become a source of merits.

I allow this struggle against the thoughts that assault you, this struggle that overwhelms you, because it glorifies Me and gives souls to Me. Offer it to Me every instant: "For You, and for souls." I change these thoughts that you do not want, that continually try you when you are asleep or awake to prevent you from loving, into graces and blessings for souls.

As you can see, it's the enemy that prevents you from accomplishing a ceaseless act of love. That is the reason for your perpetual struggle against thoughts; even good thoughts can serve as a weapon to prevent you from loving.

The virginity of the spirit makes you become beautiful and immaculate; the act of love makes you become ardent as I want you to be.

Answers to a Few Questions

37. Doesn't the exercise of a ceaseless act of love risk becoming an obsession for the spirit?

1. That exercising a ceaseless act of love requires uncommon will power and energy, and consequently, is costly to human nature, is undeniable. But it mustn't be forgotten that in practicing spiritual asceticism, everything is costly, even a single step in virtue. Jesus didn't present the ceaseless act of love to Sr. Consolata as a solace, but as a cross, upon which she was to live her vocation as victim of love, upon which she was to complete her holocaust of love and suffering for souls.

2. We cannot affirm in an absolute manner that they are truly overwhelming for the spirit; it's necessary to discern:

   a) If these are souls that never think of God, who don't even offer a single heartbeat to Him, then yes, for them it would not only be oppressive, but completely senseless. You may as well expect a dead man to get up and walk. Such souls must begin by finding grace in a good confession.

   b) As for souls who are already trying to practice virtues, far from overwhelming the heart, on the contrary,

this act will permit them to pour themselves out in greater flights of love,
and at the same time to experience
His goodness, the unchangeable faithfulness of God.

c) When a soul makes an effort to achieve
this degree of perfect love, it finds the
most beautiful expression of its life in
the act. For the souls who are sincerely
and strongly decided to live a life of
love in all of its perfection, far from
being oppressive to their spirits, the
ceaseless act of love becomes a real
"liberation" for them. The proof is
given to us in the experience of the
"littlest" souls. Where previously, their
spirits were tortured in trying to find a
way and a means to satisfy their ardent
desire to love and to save souls, they
now feel that they are free and happy,
completely where they're supposed to
be. In the littlest way, and even more
in the ceaseless act of love, they have
found what they used to painfully try
to find elsewhere. The act of love has
so completely become the heart of
their spiritual life that they can no
longer do without it, and feel a
bottomless emptiness whenever they
fail to practice it.

3. The effort to preserve the intimacy of love
with Jesus is never as painful as the many
instances of the soul's centering in on itself,

of unsatisfied and insatiable desires that cause preoccupations of all sorts, and the continual concentration on oneself. The exercise of a ceaseless act of love helps the soul to free itself from all of its shackles. These are the shackles that make the spiritual life burdensome, but not the intimacy of love with Jesus.

4. For the rest, Jesus doesn't require the same degree of perfection in this act of love from all souls, even from the "very little" ones. There are an infinity of degrees in the perfection of love. What's more, Jesus asks the great majority of souls that it be practiced only in the form of frequency.

38. Doesn't the ceaseless act of love risk obstructing the action of grace in the soul?

1. It's a mistake to think that exercising a ceaseless act of love could be an obstacle, even a small one, for the action of grace in the soul. The opposite is true.

2. Every act of love is already, in itself, the fruit of grace: inspired by grace and carried out with its help[16]. It follows that exercising a ceaseless act of love is, in itself, a ceaseless exercise of correspondence with grace.

---

[16] "Not that we're competent in ourselves to claim anything for ourselves, but our competence comes from God." (II Cor. 3:5)

3. If every act of perfect love already draws God, the Author and Giver of grace (John 14:23), to the soul, what can be said about the soul that drives itself to make a ceaseless act of perfect love out of its day?

4. The first and indispensable condition for the soul's bearing much fruit of sanctification is its union with Jesus (John 15:5), and it's love that causes this union. The soul which drives itself to love ceaselessly can do no less than achieve a perfect intimacy of love with Jesus, and consequently acquire and perfect the virtues.

5. The correspondence with divine grace will be even more perfect when the soul makes an extra effort to remain wrapped up in silence with God, and will perceive the least word or inspiration of grace. What more efficient means is there besides a virginal ceaseless act of love for maintaining the soul in a virtuous internal and external silence, in this continual vigilance of love?

6. Of herself, Sr. Consolata was able to state that during her religious life as a capuchin, she had never said "no" to God, and she had never allowed a single inspiration of grace to pass uselessly. Her life is there precisely to show the marvels that grace can work in a soul that strives to keep itself ceaselessly united to Jesus through love.

39. Doesn't exercising the ceaseless act of love risk halting the free flight of the soul in its relations with God?

1. Jesus explained to Sr. Consolata: "When you pray, meditate, or talk with Me, the act of love continues." These words explicitly state to all souls that they can keep their full spiritual liberty in their relationship with God.

   It can therefore converse, speak, be open with Him in a way that pleases Him very much, all without discontinuing the act of love.

2. While insisting on the greater value of the act of love in comparison with vocal prayers, Jesus still generally left Sr. Consolata free on that point. And we know that she made the "Way of the Cross" daily, and sometimes even twice daily (morning and night) that she recited one hundred Requiems every night before bed, that she made act of grace novenas of nine Magnificats every day; and we also know about her frequent colloquies with Jesus and the Blessed Mother, her invocations to the saints in heaven, her individual prayers for those who did good to her or for all who asked her to pray for them.

3. It is therefore clear that when it is properly understood, the exercise of a ceaseless act of love does not weigh down the wings of the soul in its flights towards God. Rather, it

maintains it in its full liberty, which permits it to raise itself to higher spheres of pure love. It doesn't prevent the soul from meditating when it feels the urge; from simply fixing its attention on God when it feels called to do so; from speaking familiarly with God; from saying other prayers, etc. In all these different situations, the act of love continues, even if the spirit and heart don't remain completely centered on the "Jesus, Mary, I love You. Save souls!"

4. It would be a grace to hope that the soul, as it progresses in intimate love with God, would do an act of love (of the heart) before every other prayer formula or way of praying. The important thing is for the soul to use the act of love to remain firmly united to Jesus through all the free moments of the day.

40. Are legitimate consolations and innocent distractions permissible for the soul which consecrates itself to the exercise of the ceaseless act of love?

1. Of course. Sr. Consolata never allowed herself a voluntary absence from the communal recreations. Far from being taciturn, she showed herself to be full of life. In a few instances she composed, and even read, some poems (rhymed poetry). When the community would gather near the radio to hear the voice of the Holy Father, or to follow certain religious ceremonies, she always participated with full spiritual joy.

She loved song and willingly took part. Had she been permitted, she would voluntarily have learned the art of painting. In the parlor, with her parents or acquaintances, she was able to blend a religious reserve with easiness and amiability. She was never at a loss for spirit filled words, especially when it became necessary to recover discourses that were taking dangerous turns, etc.

2. Doesn't St. Paul tell us that we must sanctify even our mundane actions like eating, drinking, sleeping? Therefore, a restful moment, an honest recreation, can also be sanctified by love and thus transformed into love.

3. It must be remembered that divine requests are not the same for all souls, even when the souls are called to walk identical ways. What Jesus would ask from a cloistered nun, He wouldn't require in same way from a nun with an active life, and even less from a person living in the world. He doesn't even expect to get the same thing from all of those who are cloistered as He did from Sr. Consolata, like not speaking unless someone asks you a question for example (except in a case of necessity, or for charity, or convenience) even during recreation.

4. It's necessary to follow the calls of grace and not to anticipate them. The soul must ask for this grace as it grows in the perfection of

love; and to always obtain this grace, ask for renunciation of some consolations or of some of the more unnecessary distractions.

5. However, each soul which is reaching for the perfection of divine love must constantly strive to avoid becoming dissipated. The act of love is a great help in this way. An act of love (of the heart) doesn't bring any discordant notes into a recreation, doesn't ask the soul to make any excessive efforts, and meanwhile it helps maintain the soul in God's presence and thus sanctify, through love, the recreation itself.

41. What can be said about a ceaseless act of love in relation to contemplation?

1. All souls are not called to become sanctified by following the same way, just as they haven't all been given the same gifts by God.

2. If a soul has been favored by God with the gift of infused contemplation, or has arrived at acquired contemplation; if it truly benefits from this spiritual state, or it feels itself advancing in the perfection of love, let it rest on those summits without looking for other ways or means.

3. Still, the act of love could be a great help even for those souls, for example on those days when the Lord hides His presence from them, or in those numerous moments throughout the day when, because of

their various external activities, pure contemplative love becomes very difficult for a time because it is so often interrupted by the external activity.

4. Anyways, since it keeps the soul ceaselessly and virginally fixed in God, it can't be denied that exercising a ceaseless act of love supports the soul and stabilizes it in a contemplative state.

42. Which is the most perfect, "contemplating" or "loving with a real love," that is, through the act of love?

1. The grand masters of the spiritual life teach that internal prayer is a "conversation with God and a contemplation of invisible divine realities."

2. Friendship love is manifested in all of its ardent fervency in the presence of the person who is loved. This which happens in human life also takes place, and in a more noble way, in friendship love with God. From there, the Holy Spirit Who raises us to being "lovers of God" simply raises us to the "contemplation" of Him, and finally make us capable of "intimate conversation" with Him.

3. It's therefore unnecessary to establish a difference in perfection between the elements that make up the structure of the most profound internal life, but it is

necessary to see in love a most pressing invitation to contemplation, and in this a stimulation to love always more the infinitely lovable One.

4. It wouldn't be a waste of time to add that, in itself, contemplation is the "rest" of the spirit, which adores, thanks, praises and blesses while gathering the words of the Divine Master; while the necessities of life require an occupation with so many things that are more the basis of "action." In this condition, through the active and vigilant exercise of a ceaseless act of love for God, everything is accomplished for the glory of God; and under the effect of every effort to do good, the will tries to make the One Who is worthy of all praises and blessings better known, loved, and served.

A Few Thoughts

**(Excerpts from the lessons given to
Sr. Consolata by Jesus)**

Never turn your glance away from Jesus, for any reason whatsoever; then you will sail with greater celerity towards the eternal shores.

I want you perfect, I want you to be continually with Me; consequently: Jesus only! Only Me: I am sufficient. Do you really trust Me?

Close all of the doors to the senses. Let's live in intimacy, always, the two of us, alone. Deny entrance to all thought, to everything, always. The two of us, alone.

I am always faithful to My promises; so will you be, if you remain in Me. You will become faithful with everything you promise Me, to your resolutions, because what is found in the vine is also found in its branches.

You live in Me and we are one; you will bear much fruit and become powerful, because you will disappear like a drop of water in the ocean. Within you will pass My silence, My humility, My purity, My charity, My gentleness, My patience, My thirst for suffering, My zeal for souls, to want to save them at any cost.

Always remember that I alone am holy, and I can make you holy, by transfusing My holiness into you.

My holiness becomes yours, as your purity is Mine, My humility, yours. You see? I am Love, and as long as you live in love, you live in Me, but I also live in you.

You must have such mastery over your thoughts and your words that the devil can't bother you in any way, and this mastery is a gift that the act of love gives you as a favor.

As long as you love, the devil can't cause a bad thought to enter into you because all of your faculties are absorbed by love; but if you were to stop loving, that would be when he could do so. That's why you must always love.

This ceaseless act of love gives you the threefold virginity: of the body, of the heart and of the spirit.

If you efface yourself, you don't allow a thought to enter, I will think in you. If you don't speak, I Myself will speak in you. If you don't seek to do your own will, I will act within you: it will no longer be you who live, but I Who live in you.

A Cheerful "Yes" to Everything and Seeing Jesus in Everyone

43. Is ceaseless love the summary of the Very Humble Way of Love?

In the divine lessons given to Sr. Consolata, the practice of the *Very Humble Way of Love* includes two more points:

a) a cheerful "yes" in everything, seeing and dealing with Jesus in everyone;

b) a "yes" to everything out of recognition and gratitude.

44. What correlation is there between these two points?

1. Love for God cannot be separated from love for neighbor. Jesus united the two commandments "The second is like the first" (Matthew 22:39). In the first one, we love God for Himself; in the second, we love Him in our neighbor. Our neighbor is, in some way, God made visible to us, and to Whom we do good (through our neighbor). The perfection of God's love asks for the perfection of charity towards our neighbor, and is the spirit of it. As I try to not lose a

chance to make an act of love, I must also not lose a chance to make an act of charity[17].

2. To love God with the perfection required by the first commandment, I must necessarily renounce everything that gets in the way of so perfect a love; in the same way, I must strive to please God in everything by the perfect observance of His Law, and the perfect acting out of His Will in me. Also, to be perfect in charity, I must keep myself from all that could offend or hurt my neighbor, and on the contrary do all the good I can for him in opposition to my tastes, my convenience, my satisfactions, etc. In this total renouncement made because of love of God, and in this total abnegation towards one's neighbor, is found the perfection of sacrifice included in the "yes" to everything.

3. This "everything", as each person sees it, is relative to the perfection of our love for God. In practice, this is how the perfection of fraternal charity (by not missing an act of charity from one Communion to the next) and the perfection of sacrifice (by not missing a sacrifice from one Communion to the next) will become more easily obtained as the love for God becomes more perfect in the soul (by not missing an act of love from one Communion to the next).

---

[17] "How can he who doesn't love the brother he can see, love the God Whom he cannot see?" (1 John 4:20).

45. Why "see" Jesus in our neighbor?

Because our neighbor is made in the image and likeness of God, and because Jesus identified Himself with our neighbor[18].

46. To "see Jesus" in our neighbor, is it necessary to exercise Christian charity?

It is necessary as the supernatural beginning and end of our act of charity. If our act of charity springs from a purely human origin, it can't have a supernatural value and therefore, an eternal Life[19].

47. In practice, how does one "see Jesus" in one's neighbor?

It's done by addressing all of the good that we do to our neighbor to Jesus, by doing it solely for Him.

48. Why is it said that we must see Jesus "in everyone"?

Because charity is universal. If I exclude anyone from my charity, be it a single soul or a single brother, my charity is no longer perfect.

---

[18] "I tell you the truth, every time you have done something to the least of your brothers, you have done it to Me" (Matt. 25:40).
[19] "Love ponders no evil" (I Cor. 13:5).

49. How is it possible to see Jesus in our brothers who have serious faults?

1. If we exclude our brothers who have serious faults from this vision of faith we would no longer be able to be charitable because, unfortunately, no one is without faults, and by that simple fact it would no longer be possible to exercise Christian charity.

2. Because it's faith that lets us see Jesus in everyone. He even, without making any exceptions, identified Himself with prisoners ("I was in prison, and you visited Me"). Likewise, I don't balk at the diminutive size of the consecrated Host and through faith, I believe that it completely contains Jesus; and as even the poor workmanship of a crucifix doesn't prevent me from giving Him the homage due Him, in the same way, in the exercise of charity, my faith makes me see Jesus in all my brothers, whatever their condition.

3. Note: we don' t need to see Jesus in the faults of our neighbor, but on the contrary, see the Jesus Who allows such faults to render our faith and charity more meritorious.

50. What does "deal with" Jesus in our neighbor mean?

It means that I must treat my neighbor in the same way as I would treat Jesus in person, and do it in this way:

1.	Always esteem and respect my neighbor. Even if I must reproach or disapprove of his actions, I must always respect his person.

2.	Avoid with extreme prudence all that could, in one way or another, risk being an offense against charity: In my thoughts[20], in my judgments[21], in my words[22], in my conversations[23].

51. Why is it said: deal with Jesus "in everyone"?

1.	That means that we must treat everyone well, whoever they are: our betters as our equals and our inferiors, the rich as the poor, the intelligent as the ignorant[24].

---

[20] "Love ponder no evil" (1 Cor 13:5).

[21] "Do not judge" (Matt. 7:1).

[22] "But I tell you that anyone who is angry with his brother without cause will be subject to judgment. Again, anyone who says to his brother, Raca, is answerable to the Sanhedrin. But anyone who says, "You fool!" will be in danger of the fire of hell" (Matt. 5:22). "Brothers, do not slander one another" (James 12:11).

[23] "Be devoted to one another in brotherly love. Honor one another above yourselves" (Romans 12:10).

[24] "My brothers, as believers in our glorious Lord Jesus Christ, don't show favoritism. Suppose a man comes into your meeting wearing a gold ring and fine clothes, and a poor man in shabby clothes also comes in. If you show special attention to the man

2.   That we must, besides that, treat well not only those who interest us and are good to us, but also strangers and those we haven't heard anything good about[25].

3.   And to do this all the time, not only when it's easy but also when, because of various spiritual circumstances, it costs us greatly.

52. What does practicing this "yes" require of us?

1.   That our charity grow to include acts and doesn't stop at noble sentiments and kind words[26].

2.   That we never refuse to do a favor, render a service, lend a hand to our brothers in need, each and every time that we are not

---

wearing fine clothes and say, 'Here is a good seat for you,' but say to the poor man, 'You stand there' or 'Sit on the floor by my feet,' have you not discriminated among yourselves and become judges with evil thoughts?" (James 2:1-4).

[25] "If you love those who love you, what reward will you get? Are not even the tax collectors doing that? And if you greet only your brothers, what are you doing more than others? Do not even pagans do that?" (Matt. 5:46-47).

[26] "If anyone has material possessions and sees his brother in need but has no pity on him, how can the love of God be in him? Dear children, let us not love with words or tongue but with actions and in truth" (I John 3:17-18).

physically or morally prevented from doing so. In these latter situations our refusal must be so charitably expressed that it is well accepted, without reservations.

3. That we be at our neighbor's service with solicitude and promptness in foreseeing his worries and pains, within the limits of what is possible and convenient.

53. What does this yes in "everything" include?

In the same way as we must not make exceptions in our good will towards our neighbor, we also must not make exceptions in our good will towards anyone. We must do good to everyone, without regard for whether the person who is asking for help, or the one to whom we are doing good, is attractive or homely, is worthy or unworthy, is just or unjust, is friend or foe. We must not only forgive offenses but also love and do good to the offender. That's Mercy: the sublime summit of charity, proposed by our Lord Jesus Christ through His example and His instruction (Matthew 5:39 and following):

"But I tell you, do not resist an evil person. If someone strikes you on the right cheek, turn to him the other also. And if someone wants to sue you and take your tunic, let him have your cloak as well. If someone forces you to go one mile, go with him two miles. But I tell you: love your enemies, bless those who curse you, do good to those who hate you and pray for those who persecute you, that you may be sons of your

Father in heaven. He causes His sun to rise on the evil and the good, and sends rain on the righteous and the unrighteous. Be perfect, therefore, as your heavenly Father is perfect."

54. What does a "cheerful" yes mean?

1. That charity must be done voluntarily, in all ways, and that when we give, we must do so without humiliating the recipient.

2. That we must rejoice and feel that we are sweetly and holily happy to ease, to help, to comfort the person of Jesus in our neighbor. "If you knew the gift of God and Who it is Who asks you for a drink!" (John 4:10).

3. That our facial expressions must always be loving, radiating the extreme goodness and gentle condescension of Jesus' Heart.

4. That we must rejoice with those who rejoice, suffer with those who suffer, in order to render more complete the joy of our brothers and less sorrowful their suffering.

5. Finally, that we must be ready to suffer everything rather than cause suffering to our neighbor.

A Few Thoughts

**(Excerpts from the lessons given to
Sr. Consolata by Jesus)**

The Sister, whoever she is, must no longer exist for you, but only Jesus, Who is in reality present in this heart.

I give Myself to you and I give you everything, and you, give yourself entirely and give all the help you can. Be truly annihilated in an act of love towards Me and an act of charity towards your Sisters, towards everyone.

Always do everything you can, never avoid making a single sacrifice, never refuse. I will always help you to persevere in your duties towards charity.

Don't see the creature any longer, but see only the Jesus within it. If you do this, all sacrifices will become sweet. Annihilate yourself. I became a Sacrifice for you. Look: they take Me, sacrifice Me, exhibit Me, abandon Me, they do whatever they want with Me. Do the same yourself! Let your Sisters do whatever they want with you.

There's so much to do and so urgently... and you see a Sister who needs help... Oh! Don't pass her by, but stop! Make this act of charity, and I will see to it that you arrive on time to do your duty.

Don't be afraid to exaggerate condescension, thus showing in your behavior and words how good and condescending I am.

While completely forgetting yourself, give yourself to everyone with an ever present smile. Don't omit a single act of love for Me, nor an act of charity for your Sisters and your neighbor.

Don't omit a single act of love for Me, see Me in everyone and say a resolute "yes" to all, with firm confidence that My help will never fail you. And smile. Always smile. I Myself will be smiling through you.

Remember that a loving glance and a sweet smile have a greater influence on a soul than the loveliest sermon. Isn't it true that feeling yourself loved and understood in a brotherly, holy manner can make the Way of Perfection seem a lighter one to travel?

I keep pain for Myself, and I give smiles to souls: you do the same.

Say "Yes" to everything
with thanksgiving

55. Who is this "yes" addressed to?

We say it to God Who has all of the rights of Creator, Lord, and Redeemer over us; Who wants and deserves to be served by us every instant of our lives, through a loving and perfect submission to His will for us, in whatever way that will is manifested.

56. What is included in this "yes"?

1. Generally, it includes our effective and affective acceptance of the divine will and of all divine dispositions that concern us.

2. For what particularly concerns our "sanctification": we must follow Jesus' action in our soul with docility and meekness, letting Him choose the road, the manner and the means to sanctify us; our part is to always say "yes," moment by moment, with a will to follow and promptness of action.

3. Concerning suffering; we should not go looking for it, but only accept it, moment by moment, from the loving hand of God. Yes, He will choose heartaches for us, and they will always be accompanied by His grace and will be the most sanctifying ones for us.

57. What is meant by "yes" to "everything"?

It means that we must never have any reservations about following God's will with our heart and actions. God wants everything and deserves everything. He also returns everything. Our perfect adherence to God's will must include:

1. Not only things of importance but also minor things, which puts more emphasis on the refinement of our love[27].

2. Not only the act of doing everything God wants, asks, sends, but also perfection in the way it's carried out: the time, the place, the manner, etc.; to do His will on earth as it is done in heaven.

3. Not only what conforms to our desires, to our tastes, but also to what contradicts them.

4. Not only what brings us joy, pleasure of some sort of satisfaction, but also the things that cause us sorrow and suffering.

58. In practice, what does faithfulness to "a yes to everything" call for?

1. The perfect observance to the law of God.

---

[27] "Whoever can be trusted with very little can also be trusted with much" (Luke 16:10).

2. The perfect carrying out of daily duties.

3. The generous and constant correspondence with grace, by trying to not allow even a single good inspiration to be wasted.

4. Gathering with love the little acts of virtue, the little sacrifices and the minute renunciations that Jesus endlessly sows in our path.

5. Accepting, moment by moment the choices that God makes concerning us, whether they come directly from Him, or through events, or our neighbor.

6. Accepting, day by day, whatever trials He will choose to send our way; in our body, in our heart, or in our spirit.

59. What is meant by a "grateful" yes?

It means the perfection with which we must accept and follow the divine Will:

> a) without complaint;
> b) with love;
> c) with a joyful will;
> d) with gratitude.

60. Why even with gratitude?

1. Because, whatever choices God makes concerning us, they are always the work of His infinite goodness and of His

inexhaustible merciful love, so they are always for our greatest good.

2. In particular, concerning suffering:

a) through it, Jesus has shown us His special love, "As My Father has loved Me (by crucifying Me), so have I loved you." (John 15:9)

b) through it, Jesus gives us the means to prove our love for Him;

c) through it, He purifies us and makes us do our purgatory while on earth;

d) through it, He sanctifies us and fills our brief existence here with merit;

e) through it, He makes us cooperate with the salvation of souls;

61. *Would our tears be contrary to a "yes to everything"?*

No, no more than the prayers we make, asking God to deliver us from some suffering, as long as our will always remains fully submitted to God's will. "Father, if it's possible, take this cup away from Me. Yet, not as I will but as You will" (Matthew 26:39).

62. Does the "yes to everything" take into consideration the state of the victim?

The "yes to everything" doesn't exact from the soul a particular self offering as a victim, if God Himself doesn't intervene to claim it. Yet, if we practice in a perfect way the "yes to everything," we in fact achieve the state of victim, following the Divine Victim, and united with Him, to the end of the Redemption of the world.

A Few Thoughts

**(Excerpts from the lessons given to
Sr. Consolata by Jesus.)**

*Always remain faithful to your act of love, strive to
not waste a single one, and to not omit a single act of
charity. Gather with love the flowers of virtue that I
cause to spring up on your path, and the fruit that
you bear will be abundant.*

*Holiness is forgetting yourself in everything;
thoughts, desires, words. Let Me do everything: I will
do it all, and you, moment by moment, with great
love give Me what I ask of you.*

*I have rights on you, and you, you only have one:
obeying Me. I need a docile will which allows Me to
do everything, which lends itself to everything, which
relies on Me and always serves Me, in all
circumstances, with peace and joy.*

*Let Me do what I want. Recognize that I alone exist;
there's nothing left of you but your continual act of
love and your great docility in doing, simply and
always, what I want directly or indirectly through
your Superiors and your Sisters.*

*To maintain a continual act of love in your heart, for
it to be not interrupted, it is necessary to always burn
within it the sacrificial fire, fed by continuous little
acts of virtue. It's not enough to give everything: it's*

necessary to not take anything back again, to accept everything and suffer everything for the love of Jesus.

The generosity I expect from you is the acceptance of suffering, minute by minute; suffering, not sought after, but accepted as I accepted it Myself.

Yes, suffering is the most desirable thing on earth once you understand its value, you see that you can really prove your love for God through it, and finally, that it's like money with which you can buy the salvation of souls.

Remember, the greater your sorrow will be, the more you will know that I love you. Always remember that I will manifest the intensity of My love for you through the intensity of the suffering I send you.

Remember and hold as certain that along with each burden, I will also send the strength to carry it; so, don't be afraid of anything. I love you, and I never stop thinking of you; you, preoccupy yourself with always loving Me.

Love only Me, love Me always; with a great love, answer "yes" to all and to everything, always: there is your path. Nothing but that; it is I who will think about and provide for all of the rest!

The "Littlest Way of Love" and the Apostolate

63. What can be said about the "Littlest Way of Love" relative to the Apostolate?

The "Littlest Way of Love" has an eminently apostolic character and end. True love can't be given without zeal, and true zeal doesn't exist without love. In the "Littlest Way of Love," love and zeal attract one another, and reciprocally complete and perfect one another.

64. From what is this apostolic character deduced?

1. From the immediate end of the "Littlest What of Love," which is to transport the soul to the most perfect intimacy with Jesus. This end, by divine promise, is an assurance of a great abundance of spiritual fruit: sanctification and souls (John 15:5).

2. From the formula of the ceaseless act of love, which is the foundation for the Littlest Way of Love: "Jesus, Mary, I love You. Save Souls!" Love and souls: a mixture of harmonious contemplation and action, and a ceaseless pulsation of love for God and of charity for one's neighbor.

3. The fact that, in this formula, Jesus has united a properly spoken act of love, "Jesus, Mary, I

love You.," with a petition in favor of souls, "Save Souls!", tends to show that love is ceaselessly given to Jesus (Redeemer) and to the Most Holy Virgin Mary (Co-Redemptrix) to obtain salvation for souls. If we consider the value of the prayer in general, and the love at the end of the apostolate in particular, it will be easy to understand the universal reality of the apostolate which is exercised by the soul who is heroically faithful to the "Littlest Way of Love."

4.   The great promises which Jesus made to Sr. Consolata concerning her apostolate in favor of souls are another proof of the goals and of the apostolic efficacy of the "Littlest Way of Love."

65. What can be said about the "yes to everything" relative to the Apostolate?

The "yes to everything" through which the soul lovingly accepts all God's decisions concerning it, and embraces a daily cross with love, is, in itself, a testimony of love for God and a cooperation for the salvation of souls. Like all acts of love, so are all sorrows offered to God for souls. Therefore, a "yes to everything" for souls.

66. Why say "universal Apostolate?"

1.   Because, as it was explained in its proper section, the "save souls" of the ceaseless act of love includes all the souls of the universe and of all time, and all their necessities. In

union with Jesus, the "Littlest Way" embraces the world of souls; it loves, prays and suffers for all the souls which have been created or are yet to be, till the end of the ages; it claims Sr. Consolata's heroic agenda: "ALL the love and ALL the sorrows for ALL the souls."

2. Concerning the souls in purgatory, the "save souls" has a particular significance: obtaining divine Mercy that purgatory be dispensed with, or that it be shortened.

67. Will the "Littlest Way of Love" be a reflection of good for the whole world?

The "Littlest Way of Love" was unveiled by Jesus for Sr. Consolata with the intention of forming an army of souls consecrated to love for the renewal of the world through love and charity: summary of the Law.

A Few Thoughts

(Excerpts from the lessons given to
Sr. Consolata by Jesus)

Love Me for each and every one of My creatures, for each and every heart which exists. I am so thirsty for love!

Yes, ask forgiveness for poor guilty humanity, ask for the triumph of My Mercy for them, but especially, ask, Oh! Ask for an outpouring upon them of the embrace of divine Love which, like a new Pentecost, delivers mankind from its illnesses.

Ask Me for love, the triumph of My love for you, for each soul on earth, those that exist now, and those that will exist until the end of the ages. Love Me for all of them and, through your prayers and your sacrifice, prepare the world for the coming of My love.

Since you are thirsting to love Me and to save souls, always remain in Me, never leave Me for one instant and you will reap much fruit.

Consider St. Peter: alone, he had fished all night and hadn't caught a thing; with Me, he had barely thrown in the nets before they were full of fish. In the same way, if you remain in Me, with each inspiration for mortification that I send you, you will throw in the nets and I will pull them in, full of souls which you will only know in Paradise.

The fruitfulness and value of the act of love for saving souls will only be known in Paradise.

Does the cross that I've given you please you? It's very fruitful! The cross of love is more fruitful than any other cross for Me and for souls.

You, think only of Me and of souls: of Me, to love Me; of souls, to save them. I am thirsty, thirsty for souls, and that's the reason for your love and your pain.

Without sacrifice, without physical, moral, spiritual suffering, you will not save souls. But you will obtain the conversion of souls through a ceaseless pulsation of love, a ceaseless pulsation of pain.

I saved souls through the martyrdom of love, martyrdom of pain; and you will also save them that way.

The work of the "Littlest Souls"

I. The Littlest Souls

68. What are the "littlest souls"?

They are souls called to follow the littlest way of love which was shown to Sr. Consolata Betrone by Jesus.

69. Do they need a special vocation?

1. Before all else, it is necessary to have the vocation of which St. Paul speaks when he asks the faithful of Ephesus to live in a manner worthy of the "vocation" to which they had been called (Ephesians 4:1). He's not only speaking of a vocation to faith, but he invites the Christians to remain faithful to their vocation and to make good use of the gifts of God. A Christian is one who daily answers this divine call and regulates his behavior in such a way as to conform to the requirements of this calling, by making an effort to correspond with it more and more closely. Jesus reveals and manifests the ways and means which are more apt to help in advancing on the road of eternal salvation to those souls which are dear to Him so that they can become perfect in love.

2. When Sr. Consolata receives this divine illumination in her heart and communicates it to souls, these souls, having already been

called by Jesus to a Christian life or to the religious life, are concurrently invited and called to grow in love. It's in this sense that we can speak about a special vocation to love; and this vocation, although already included in the Christian vocation, will nevertheless develop and become a reality in a different way in each soul, which will conform to the soul's life conditions.

3. This shows up often in the numerous lessons which Sr. Consolata receives from Jesus. Here is an example: "If you believe that I'm omnipotent, then believe that I'm able to give you this continual act of love: I want to do it."

And so, Jesus alone can give a soul the grace to be able to persevere in the ceaseless act of love. When Jesus wants a soul to achieve the perfection of love through the ceaseless act of love, He gives the soul that grace.

70. Are these souls numerous?

1. Their number? Only Jesus knows that. Because only He knows those who belong to Him and have given themselves to Him completely. It's a consolation to think that Jesus speaks of thousands and thousands of souls who love Him and will love Him in this way.

2. Let's desire not so much to discover the exact number of these souls as to live in such

74

a way as to extend this family, and to rejoice in the thought that the friends of God can become more and more numerous at all times and places.

71. What formalities must be observed to become a part of these "littlest souls"?

None. No induction, no insignia, nothing of this sort. There are no associations, no companies, etc., but there is a spiritual way which is open to all souls who feel drawn to embrace it.

72. Isn't there at least some special consecration required?

It's natural for the soul who feels drawn to walk this path to experience a need to begin with some sort of consecration to love. The very first of the littlest souls did this, as well as the others who have become a part of this privileged society.

73. How is this consecration made?

There's no established ceremony. Taking the example of the first "littlest soul," we recommend:

a) set a date, preferably a feast of Our Lord or the Blessed Mother or even a First Friday of the month;

b) prepare for it with a few days of quiet and prayer;

c) attend Mass and receive Holy Communion on the set date, make the consecration of the "littlest souls," entrusting yourself to the Sacred Heart of Jesus through the hands of the Blessed Mother;

d) end with the recitation of the Magnificat.

74. Is it necessary to use a special formula for a consecration?

No, the soul is free to express its own commitment to the Littlest Way of Love, in whatever manner it finds the most pleasant and however the heart dictates.

75. Nevertheless, couldn't you suggest a formula?

Yes, but always leaving the soul completely free to modify or add what it will. The following is a suggestion:

"Sacred Heart of Jesus, Who has so loved men and Who asks nothing but love in return, I, ..., anxious to satisfy the ardent desire of Your Divine Heart, through the Hands of Immaculate Mary consecrate myself to You as a littlest soul, promising to strive to transform my entire life into a virginal, ceaseless act of love, which includes a cheerful "yes" to everyone, and a grateful "yes" to everything. Accept, O good Jesus, my consecration; bathe it in Your Precious Blood and transform it with Your omnipotent grace, that I may be faithful to it until death, and that this ceaseless act of love, begun here on earth, may continue for an eternity in Heaven. Heart of Jesus, so thirsty for love and for souls, make of me Your littlest host of love, that I might co-operate with You and our Most Holy Mother for the salvation of souls. Amen."

76. Is this sort of consecration binding under pain of sin?

Absolutely not. Neither mortal sin, nor venial sin. Nothing. Abandoning this way or neglecting the ceaseless act of love simply deprives the individual of the merits and the fruits of the omitted acts.

77. Is it good to renew the act of consecration?

It's good to renew it on the anniversary date, and in other particular circumstances.

78. How should the soul who feels drawn to this way proceed?

It's necessary to proceed slowly, with calm and reflection, to ensure that this impulse is really the fruit of God's grace and not of some fleeting enthusiasm. For that, it would be good to ask for

God's enlightenment with a fervent prayer and also to practice for a certain amount of time, without a formal consecration, the three points of the Littlest Way of Love, especially that which concerns the act of ceaseless love. It's only after such reassurance that the heart and spirit are ready and that the soul receives real help for its life within, that it will be ready to make a consecration to the Littlest Way.

79. Generally speaking, what rule should a spiritual director follow?

1. It would be a mistake to believe that a director can push large numbers of souls from among those he directs into following this way, even if they were all good and pious. Besides, it's not the number that counts. In the same way as Jesus needs victim souls who are such in fact and not simply in name, so does He want Littlest souls who really are such, and not only in name.

2. Contrarily, the spiritual director will find that a greater number of souls will desire and be ready to use the act of love as a means to sustain and develop their spiritual life without, however, trying to practice it ceaselessly, as we will see in the next paragraph.

80. Is it necessary for the spiritual Father to follow the same way as the "Littlest Souls" himself?

It's certainly desirable, but not necessary. It's sufficient for him to know what it's all about, so that he can help the soul to sanctify itself in the way of love.

81. What errors can the "Littlest Souls" expose themselves to?

Especially in the beginning, they can be the victims of several illusions and errors, which the devil the adversary of love can use to discourage them.

1. It would be an illusion to think that it's necessary to do everything Sr. Consolata was doing, or to imagine that we can attain the perfection that she achieved with the continuity of the act of love. Besides the different states and conditions of life, it's necessary to remember that Sr. Consolata received some very special graces and gifts which were inherent to her particular mission. The "Way" is identical in itself for all the littlest souls, but not everyone is called to make the same progress in it. When a soul is doing all it can, it attains the goal which God wants from it.

2. It would be an illusion to expect to arrive at continuity in the act of love in a short time.

Remember that Sr. Consolata, in spite of the gifts she received from God, had to be content with a moral continuity of will and effort for at least ten years.

3.   It's an illusion to believe that the exercise of the ceaseless act of love doesn't cost the soul anything. We've said it before, but it needs to be said again: it's a cross, but a sanctifying one; it's an immolation of all the senses; it is the death of nature for the triumph of grace.

4.   It's an illusion to expect that the enormous things promised to the littlest souls by Jesus consists of extraordinary gifts, charisms, etc. No, they rather consist of the summits of sanctity which are attained by souls through love and suffering. They also have nothing to do with spiritual sweetness, but are compatible with joys of the heart and the profound peace of spirit which, even in the midst of the greatest agonies, made Sr. Consolata say, "I am happy, happy, happy!"

5.   It's a mistake to believe that the act of love is less fervent or agreeable to God when it's continued in disgust, boredom, or as if by force. An act of love which is offered in such circumstances of spirit can have as much value as ten or even one hundred which were done with a felt fervor.

6.   It's a mistake to think that after an infidelity or an omission that the act of love is no longer sincere and it loses its value; it's even

a means or putting things back into place, regaining the time which was lost and going forward.

82. How must they proceed with exercising the ceaseless act of love?

1. With an energetic will, yes, but also with great calm, peace and pleasantness. Bit by bit, the act of love must become a need for the spirit, and a joy for the heart, not a torment. It's true that it's a cross, especially during times of spiritual dryness, but, as Jesus explained to Sr. Consolata, it's a cross which helps to support all other crosses.

2. Little souls, to use the expression, place their hand in Jesus' and let Him lead them through the daily events, even the most tiny and inconsequential ones, as they remain focused on Him, loving Him. Yet again, if you will, the littlest soul has built a dwelling in the Heart of Jesus and abides there, in silence and recollection, attentive and vigilant, so that not a single act of love, a single act of charity, a single act of virtue or a sacrifice will be passed up.

3. But all that, always with calm, without agitation, without even becoming excited, or even less, becoming bothered over one's own problems and infidelities, always ready to take up the song of love again after each interruption which was more or less deliberate, more or less drawn out.

83. What means can the soul use to help with the exercise of the ceaseless act of love?

1. The greater help is prayer. As the life of Sr. Consolata was a ceaseless act of love, she also made it into a ceaseless prayer to obtain a heroic faithfulness to the Littlest Way of Love from God.

2. Among other means mentioned in various parts of this little book, let's reiterate the following points:

    a) renewing the resolution of the ceaseless act of love daily, in Holy Communion;

    b) renewing it each hour of the day, as Jesus suggested to Sr. Consolata;

    c) use it (and the other two points of the Littlest Way of Love) as the basis for self examination;

    d) to live in the present moment, sanctifying it with love and through a generous adherence to God's will, without being preoccupied with the next moment.

3. The soul can also help itself with pious maxims on the value of the act of love, for example: "Each act of love lasts eternally... Each act of love is one soul... Each act of love

increases my love for Jesus and Jesus' love for me... Each act of love is worth infinitely more than all of the treasures on earth... The act of love helps me to put a maximum value on every instant of the day, etc."

84. What are the spiritual characteristics of the "Littlest Souls?"

1. The usual traits of a Littlest Soul are: confidence and abandon. These two holy traits are like a consequence and a perfection of the life of love.

2. Among the moral virtues which must come to light: humility and charity in a spirit of sacrifice and zeal.

85. What can be said about the "Littlest Way of Love" in relation to the spirit of the various religious congregations?

1. In the same way as little Theresa's "Little Way of Love," when considered in it's essence, can't be in opposition to the spirit of any religious congregation, so it is with the "Littlest Way of Love." It's the same spirit from one part or another spiritual childhood drawn from the Gospel and concretized here in the three points explained above.

2. The primary and essential aim of religious life consists in the concentration of all one's strength towards perfection of charity, or divine love, through voluntary detachment

from everything (poverty), everyone (chastity), and oneself (obedience). How could a doctrine, a spiritual life whose goal is precisely to make the soul rise higher in the perfection of love, through the perfection of charity, sacrifice, and self-renunciation, be in opposition to all of that?

3. The particular aim of each individual congregation is the one which is set by the Rule or the Constitutions, and applied to various daily activities by the Directory. So, in the Littlest Way of Love, nothing is required of the soul which is opposed to the Rule, nothing is added to the Rule, but only the Rule itself in all of its outer perfection (in execution), and inner perfection (in purity of intention, love). Sr. Consolata summarized her religious life's practical agenda in these three words: "the Rule, duty, love." And Jesus confirmed it for her: "The ceaseless act of love will bring you to the scrupulous observation of every point of the Rule, the Constitutions and the Directory."

4. If all the members of each religious community were to try to put the agenda of the Littlest Way of Love into the practice, "to not omit a single act of love, a single act of charity, a single act of virtue, a single sacrifice from one Communion to the next," how could the spirit of the Congregation itself, whatever it is, not flourish or revive?

5. That doesn't mean that all, or the majority of religious souls are called to embrace the form of the *Littlest Way of Love*. The issue is rather the "spirit" of the Littlest Way of Love, that is, cultivating a profound inner life – a life of love – through an exercise which is always more perfect in virtue and apostolate: that's what could and should be the object of all religious souls' aspirations. All can also know the value of an act of love, either within themselves, or as a means of advancing in a life of love.

86. Could you suggest a special prayer for "littlest souls" to us?

We suggest this: "O Jesus, You Who love the small and humble with a special love, and Who reveal Your secrets of love to them, change me, also me, into a littlest one, a humble one, and for the good of souls, graciously reveal, also to me, Your secrets of love. O Jesus, You Who, through an act of love, give Yourself to souls, give Yourself also to me who wants to live in love for You."

II. The "Little Angels"

87. Who are the "Little Angels?"

The term "Little Angels," like "Littlest Ones[28]," refers to souls, of course. The "Little Angels" are all the souls who, although not called to render God the essence of the act of love, ceaseless and virginal, nevertheless do use it more or less assiduously to progress in the life of love, sanctify themselves and cooperate in the salvation of souls.

88. Can children and the very young belong to the "Little Angels?"

Certainly. This was the dearest wish of Sr. Consolata's heart, the most ardent vow of her life: to lead the young to Jesus. When Jesus taught her how to practice the ceaseless act of love, and predicted that other souls would follow her, her first thought was for the young; and how happy she was to be able to give children the doctrine of the act of love through the way of the "Little Angels!"

89. Is it possible to have children learn the act of love?

Not only is it possible, but it's not hard. Isn't it written, "From the mouths of children and infants You have ordained praise" (Psalm 8:2)?

---

[28] Or "Littlest souls."

And wasn't this realized to the letter the moment of Jesus' triumphant entry into Jerusalem? (Matthew 21:26). This God Who has given rise to perfect praise in the hearts and on the lips of the Hebrew children will also know how to give rise to the act of love, the true perfect praise, in the heart and on the lips of Christian children. [29]

90. How does one proceed with children?

It's necessary to proceed by degrees: first of all, to teach them the act of love, abbreviated in the words, "Jesus, I love You," and then, "Jesus, Mary, I love You," only the older ones should be made to repeat the complete formula: "Jesus, Mary, I love You! Save souls!"

91. Is it good to make young people learn the act of love?

It's a very useful thing for opening their heart to divine love, and drawing many graces upon them. If we, who are bad, never forget a proof of affection, how many benedictions will the Heart of Jesus, which is infinitely good, pour out upon these little ones who make efforts to tell Him and

---

[29] The last words of Guy of Fongalland, on his deathbed, were: "Jesus, I love You!" In the life of little Maria Filipetto (1912-1927), these words are recorded: "Jesus, I love You! I can't say anything else. Let every beat of my heart be a throb of love for You!" Little Jacinta of Fatima used to say, "I love Jesus and the Madonna so much that I never tire of telling Them that I love Them!"

repeat to Him that they love Him? When they grow up, they won't forget the act of love which will be a precious help throughout their life and at the moment of their death.

92. Whose duty is this?

All those who have a ministry to children: mothers, religious sisters, teachers, Catholic Action members, etc. Further on, we will print Sr. Consolata's invitation to the "Littlest Souls" on this subject.

93. Can adults take part in the "Little Angels?"

Having already explained that Jesus OFFERS the act of love, we will be content to repeat often that He offers it to souls of good will.

1. Consecrated souls who don't feel drawn to take part in the "Littlest Souls" will always be able to practice, with great profit, the act of love (which is an internal act) especially for combating the dissipation of the spirit and its self-absorption.

2. The laity, who are taken up with the necessities of life and don't have the time to say long prayers, can find that the act of love is a great help in their spiritual life, to sanctify their daily fatigue and allow them to pray longer without having it interrupt their activity.

3. The sick can gather incalculable advantages from exercising the act of love: to sanctify their suffering, and sometimes make up for all of the prayers or pious exercises that would otherwise be impossible because of their disease. Occasionally repeating an act of love, while lifting their spirit to thoughts of faith and hope which comforts them, with the certainty of cooperating with the salvation of souls in this way, draws the compassionate glance of the Heart of Jesus and the maternal tenderness of His Mother upon them.

4. The elderly, for whom it's impossible to make great sacrifices or grand actions, perhaps even reduced to inactivity, can find a powerful help in the exercise of the act of love and an easy way to give value for themselves and for souls to their last years of life, and maybe even regain lost time through the intensity of their spiritual life. This explains why the elderly accepted the doctrine of the act of love so favorably and received it with such great spiritual satisfaction.

94. Is a special consecration necessary in order to belong to the "Little Angels?"

No, because the "Little Angels" don't embrace a particular spiritual life, but simply a particular way of praying, which makes use of the act of love (even as an invocation) in whatever measure possible.

95. In what sense can the act of love be called ceaseless in relation to the "Little Angels?"

In the sense that, although it isn't ceaseless through the action of a single person, it remains such as long as it is done by a number of people, the number itself being more or less important. If there are a certain number of people in a community, or in a parish, who frequently repeat the act of love, then a ceaseless act of love will continually rise to Heaven from this community, this parish, and will come back down upon them in a rain of graces and blessings.

III. The Work

96. What is understood by "The Work of the Littlest Souls?"

1. The work of the Littlest Souls, promised to Sr. Consolata by Jesus, has the goal of keeping alive and developing the Littlest Way of Love in the world by grouping together the Littlest Souls and the Little Angels.

97. So the "Littlest Way of Love" must continue in the world?

It seems so. Sr. Consolata received a promise from Heaven that the Littlest Souls and the Little Angels would live in the bosom of the Church until the end of time.

98. Does the Work have the joy of being a special organization?

It's evident that it must have its own organization, oriented on the goal it's pursuing.

99. What is this organization?

It's not yet possible to determine the precise form under which this organization will present itself. But it seems that it will need a Center of inner and outer activity: its goal being to cause love to radiate out into the world, through the means of the Littlest Way, intensely lived and propagated.

A Few Thoughts

**(Excerpts from the lessons given to
Sr. Consolata by Jesus)**

Among the Benjamins of Catholic Action there are the "Littlest Ones," and there are also some among the little souls. You are part of them, and the souls who will follow you will also belong to them, to give Me a ceaseless act of love.

You remember your great mission: give the little ones to Jesus and Jesus to the little one? Well! Even in Heaven you will present Me with little ones, the littlest ones, and you will give Me to them through a ceaseless act of love.

When your last "Jesus, Mary, I love You!" will have been pronounced, I will gather it up, and through the writings about your life, I will transmit it to thousands of sinful souls who will receive and follow it in the simplicity of this way of confidence and love, and they will thus love Me.

The Littlest Souls will be numerous, so numerous; not just thousands, but millions and millions! They will not all be women; men will also take part. Oh yes there are even many Littlest Souls among men!

After your death, the Littlest Souls will hasten towards you, just as one day, noticing you were at St. Maxim's, the little ones at the catechism, the Benjamins, hastened towards you.

I want a wave of love to surge from the earth to Heaven. You yourself must blaze the trail of the Littlest Way. One day you will serve as a model: as the world has its eyes fixed on St. Theresa today, so will the millions of Littlest Souls turn towards you.

Yes, the hearts of the Littlest Souls are destined to die of love for Me, to be consumed exclusively for Me. The world doesn't have the right to call Me cruel, because such a great number will die in sin, victims of the world! Isn't it therefore just that a creature should consume itself for its Creator?

Forget yourself, don't think of yourself or of the concerns of your special vocation. No, the Heart of Jesus has used you as an instrument (as you use a broom), but the One Who will accomplish the marvelous Work of the Littlest Souls is Him, exclusively Him.

Yes, the Littlest Souls are the pupil of My Eyes.

A Letter From Sr. Consolata to the "Littlest Souls"

Dearest "Littlest Soul,"

At night, when you are getting ready to go to bed, make sure you pray to your good guardian angel, asking him to love Jesus for you while you sleep, and to inspire the act of love into you when he awakens you in the morning. If you are faithful to praying in this way every night, he will be faithful, every morning, to awakening you with a "Jesus, Mary, I love You! Save Souls!"

With your day begun in this way, you will continue it by loving, and by approaching the Eucharistic Jesus. However, this doesn't mean that you must abandon every other prayer; no, continue your usual pious practices without adding any new ones, but let the act of love absorb all of your free time. Afterwards, if Jesus moves you, you can even say some vocal prayers.

In Holy Communion, confide and abandon your person, your preoccupations, your projects, your desires, and your sorrows to Jesus, and don't think about them any longer. Because the whole life of a "Littlest Soul" is based on the divine promise "I will think of everything; you think only of loving Me." (Copy these words onto an icon and the Sacred Heart, and try to have them always present in your spirit; they will be a great help to you, for freeing your spirit from all preoccupations, and they will be a proof, through experience, that Jesus is faithful to this promise.)

After having abandoned everything to Jesus in Holy Communion, renew your promise of the ceaseless act of love, the "Yes to everything" He will ask of you throughout the day, and the resolution to see Him, speak to Him, and serve Him with love in all creatures you will have to deal with.

Once and for all, intend to direct your entire act of love towards Heaven, and beg Him to grant you the faithfulness to live it out until your next Communion, that it may thus be the reparation for your infidelities.

You will leave church having begun your act of love, and you will continue it in transit, at home, wherever your duty binds you. Rest assured that Jesus promised that when you write, pray, or speak from necessity or for charity, the act of love continues just the same.

On your work (for example, on your stitching) or at your place of work, try to keep the words, written on an icon or a card, "Jesus, Mary, I love You! Save souls!" in plain sight. It will serve as a reminder.

From among the obstacles to the ceaseless act of virginal love you owe Jesus, He teaches you to combat three: thoughts, discussions, useless attachments. Thoughts, preoccupations: all become useless from the moment Jesus promises his "Littlest Soul" that He will think of everything, right up to the tiniest details. Useless conversations: if you speak beyond what concerns duty, charity, politeness, it's wasted time, stolen from love. Attachments, curiosities, etc., everything, in short, which distracts your spirit from the single thing it must remain devoted to: loving Jesus, ceaselessly, with a virginal love.

Meanwhile, it's necessary for you to admit that in order to realize the divine desires, "one must not omit a single act of love or any of charity, from one Communion to the next," and that the work of your soul, carried along by grace, will be lengthy and continue to require constant and generous efforts, especially without discouragement, for a long time. With each more or less voluntary infidelity, renew your resolution for virginal love and begin again. If this infidelity causes you to suffer, offer it to Jesus as an act of love. You will see and be aware of the tenderness with which Jesus will raise you back up after a fall or an infidelity; how He will hasten to set you back on your feet, so that you can continue your song of love.

What will be a great help for giving your being to Jesus in the ceaseless act of love will be renewing, every moment, your resolution to do it; and after that, your self examination on this resolution. Note that in the self examination, all that must be considered as failure is the time which was wasted in useless conversations, or the fantasy of useless thought, etc. Make reparation, if God wants you to, by making a cross on the ground with your tongue, and peacefully begin again with your service of love.

The resolution with which you concentrate all of your energy will always reflect on the ceaseless act of love. But don't be afraid, Jesus will always help you. He said: "Love, and you will be happy, and the more you love Me, the happier you will be!" Take courage, Jesus and Mary will help you. Don't be afraid, ever; have confidence and believe in Their love for you.

Affectionately,

Sr. M. Consolata, R.C.SR.

Consolata's Call To The "Littlest Souls" for the "Angelets" (Little Angels)

We would like to point out that Sr. Consolata reserved the term "Little Angels" for little ones, according to their age, and it came from a particular inclination of her heart.

"The day when, at the gate in the parlor, I learned that a section for "Little Angels" had been constituted in Catholic Action, I addressed this ardent, although timid, desire to God: "Jesus, to whom will You confide the direction of the 'Angelets'?" And Jesus, always good, always maternally condescending, as if He wanted to compensate me for the sacrifice of complete annihilation He asked from me concerning the "Littlest Souls," answered me within: "The Angelets will be yours, really yours. It's you I confide them to, and you will assemble them." From that moment, the Angelets were born in my heart, begotten by a very lively affection.

But how could I assemble "the Angelets" throughout the world and teach them the act of love, me, a poor contemplative nun closed up in a cloister? What is impossible for the creature isn't so for the Almighty. With complete confidence, I awaited the accomplishment of the divine promise; and so set about preparing the way with prayer.

But see, O Jesus, now You've asked me for the sacrifice of my life, and soon I will stand in Your divine Presence. O Jesus, You are the only One Who knows with what love, with what tenderness, I would have assembled the "Angelets" of the universe, to teach them how to stutter, to repeat the act of love! But here I am, coming in Your direction. Ah well! I pray, I beg You, through the heart of Your divine Mother, who is also mine, I ask You to raise up, from among the "Littlest Souls" of the entire world, from among the souls who are devoted to working with children: in the orphanages, in the schools, in the churches, in the associations, among the mothers and sisters of good families, I beg You to raise apostle's hearts from everywhere, which will try to promote the coming of Your reign of love, gathering many "Angelets" (of both genders) from those who are born to life, and teaching them the act of love.

O Jesus, I am coming to You, but, near Your divine Heart where I will love eternally, I will watch over these apostles and protect them, and through them I will assemble the "Angelets" for You from all parts of the world, while You and Your Mama, who is also mine, receive perfect praise from these innocent hearts. And that's how Your promise will be accomplished. Thank You, O my God, now and always!"

A Few Thoughts
By Sr. Consolata
Concerning the Exercise
of the Ceaseless Act of Love

I'm not always able to express myself as I would wish, but I understand that in practice, an act of love gives Jesus to the soul, or increases its grace; it's like a Communion.

How the certainty that each act of love lasts eternally makes me joyful, active, vigilant! If the ceaseless act of love gives all to Jesus, it also gives everything to the soul. Yes, truly, the act of love is everything: it is light, strength and everything else.

The ceaseless act of love prepares the soul to resist temptation. It sustains the soul during temptation because love is everything.

The ceaseless act of love always maintains the soul in peace. I believe that it has a strong influence over suffering; it helps the soul to suffer with joy.

Being gathered up, I am separated from the earth. The ceaseless act of love unites me to God.

I joyfully notice that the act of virginal love transforms, raises and divinizes the soul.

To live on the Cross of the ceaseless act of love is to live in detachment from the world: God and souls, that's the realization of divine will!

For me, the most perfect sacrifice, the true holocaust, is to never omit a single act of love from awakening till sleeping.

Love and souls! Don't omit a single act of love, don't lose a single soul!

The ceaseless act of love is more powerful than any suffering: so, to place myself above suffering, I must not cease to love.

Be watchful that the thorns of preoccupations don't suffocate the act of love, and remember that it's through patience that the soul will bear the fruit to which it aspires!

Concentrate everything into this intention, into this "I will not omit a single act of love" and all of the rest will come of itself.

Everything, all strengths, all energies, all activities of the soul: all must be put to work in such a way that the act of love if never interrupted. Nothing else should hold your attention, only the act of love. Behold my life: the act of love. It's all that Jesus has asked of me.

I desire, I always desire, with all of my strength, I desire to live the present moment; I don't want to allow a single thought, a single preoccupation to penetrate my soul. Not a single word will escape my lips, if it's not uttered out of true necessity: no nothing can make me omit a single act of love.

I desire, with all of my strength, I desire a continuous: "Jesus, Mary, I love You! Save Souls!" I want to see and deal with Jesus alone in all men. Jesus, I trust in You.

O Jesus, with Your help, I don't want to miss a single act of love, not a single one. Yes, Jesus, that's what I want! And this "I want," so that it can be faithful, I plunge it into a bath of Your divine Blood, and I leave it there forever.

It seems to me that Jesus has really rooted the ceaseless act of love within me. Throughout my continuous struggles, I use all of my strength to prevent any creature, any task, any temptation from turning me away from the act of love.

Sr. Consolata's Prayer to Obtain Heroic Faithfulness to the "Littlest Way"

Jesus, when my spirit is presented with images, thoughts, memories, please remind me that I've renounced everything for Your Love, and that I've promised You that I would keep my spirit intact, wanting only one single thought, but forever: "Jesus, Mary, I love You! Save Souls!"

Jesus, when I get the urge to express a point of view about work, or the desire to give advice, etc., please remind me that I must not interest myself in anything, except the thought of following You, of preoccupying myself only with loving You.

Jesus, when during recreation or during the hour of mandatory silence, I am tempted to speak or make confidences, please remind me that, through love of You, I have promised to hold my tongue, through the daily Eucharistic Meeting, to not speak without being questioned, and to answer only what is necessary, and always in a soft voice.

Jesus, when a wave of disgust surprises me, please remind me that in compensation for all You've done for me and for all You will yet do, that I have promised You a ceaseless act of love, that it's only by loving You with a ceaseless love that I will attain the summit, that I will be living my vocation and that I will be helping to save souls.

Jesus, when the enemy presents me with my sisters' faults, please remind me that I must not allow myself to judge or blame, but only to be compassionate, to speak and to serve and all with love.

Jesus, to do You homage with this ceaseless act of love, I have renounced everything. Ah! Don't let me lose ground, or take a thought back from You, or speak a word which could be a negation of this Love!

Prayer For Obtaining Graces Through the Intercession of Sr. Consolata

Father of all compassion, You have brought among us Your servant Sister M. Consolata Betrone to spread throughout the world the incessant love towards Your Son Jesus in the simple path of confidence and love.

Make us, too, capable, guided by Your Spirit, of being ardent witnesses of Your love and of Your immense bounty and grant us, by Your intercession, the grace which we need. For Christ our Lord. Amen.

Imprimatur
Turin, March 11 1995
+ Pier Giorgio Micchiardi

Anyone receiving graces through the intercession of Sr. Consolata Betrone is asked to give notice of them to the following address:
Monastero Sacro Cuore
Via Duca d'Aosta, 1
10024 Moncalieri (TO) Italy

www.consolatabetrone-monasterosacrocuore.it

APPENDIX

Biography of Sr. Mary Consolata
Written by the Monastery of the Sacred Heart
http://www.consolatabetrone-monasterosacrocuore.it

<u>A LIFE FOR LOVE</u>

"The life of the Saints is a rule of life for others": with these words in Turin, in the Sanctuary of Our Lady Help of Christians, on February 8 1995, Archbishop Card. Giovanni Saldarini started the canonical process for five cases of beatification. One of these was the Poor Clare nun Sister Maria Consolata Betrone. The biographical outlines of the new Servant of God, born in Saluzzo (Cuneo) on April 6 1903 and dying on July 18 1946 in the Convent of the "Sacred Heart" of Moriondo Moncalieri (Turin) could have been briefly spent behind the rise and fall of a life which only lasted 43 years, of which 17 in a strictly closed order. It could have been thus if, instead, God had not made of her brief existence an incandescent meteor of love, rich of eternity.

<u>1. THE YOUNG PIERINA</u>
Daughter of Pietro Betrone and Giuseppina Nirino, the owners of a bakery in Saluzzo (Cuneo) and then managers of a restaurant in Airasco (Turin), Pierina was the second of six daughters born of her father's second marriage.

i

She was 13 years old when the Lord cast his loving gaze on her. Indeed, one day the girl was hurrying to do her errands in the village when, unexpectedly, an intense, strange prayer flowed from her heart: "My God, I love you!". The unusual spiritual emotion overcame her. It was for her the meeting with the Lord. Years later, in her autobiographical notes, she recalls that experience with the simplicity and freshness of the moment, fixing it inside her forever.

On December 8 1916, the Feast of the Immaculate Conception, Pierina dedicated herself to the Virgin.

Receiving Holy Communion the Divine invitation was made more explicit, for she distinctly heard within her the words "Do you want to be mine?" Deeply touched by grace, she cried and "with tears, though without understanding the extent of the question, she replied, "Jesus, yes".

On February 26 1917 the Betrone family moved to Turin. Pierina was 14 years old and between family and spiritual trials, scruples and temptations and insidious and intimate sufferings she had to wait until she was 21 before being able to realize her vocation. Until then the words of the prophet in a similar story of divine seduction and salvation of the beloved, "I am going to lure her and lead her out into the wilderness and speak to her heart" (Hos. 2, 16) were uniquely true for her.

It is the inner portrait of the young Pierina. Once conquered by the Lord, she yearned for an ideal of perfection, she lived in the memory of a promise and waited for its realization.

2. CONFIDANTE OF THE LORD

"Nothing attracts me among the Capuchins", was Pierina's comment when, after three failed attempts to take the veil in open orders, she was advised by her confessor Don Accomasso, to take the decision to enter the Convent of the Poor Clares in Turin. It was April 17 1929. Effectively in her, as well as the inclination of grace through penitence, other three elements peculiar to the Franciscan order were evident: poverty, the communal life and happiness. Thus on February 28 1930 her religious Ceremony of taking the Veil took place with the name of Sister Maria Consolata. The Blessed Virgin Mary is venerated in Turin under the name of Consolata, namely Consoler of the Afflicted. The new name chosen by young Betrone is indicative, even more than of her mission, of her very existence; of being the consoler of the Heart of Jesus and of all those who are unable to perceive or welcome the love of the Lord. According to what she would present she would be "a missionary, but to the infinite". The day of the Ceremony of taking the Veil she perceives a Divine suggestion that shows her the way to it: "I do not ask you more than this: an act of continual love". And for more than 16 years of enclosed Capuchin life this would be the foundation on which will concentrate and unify her entire being, molding herself to it at every moment of her existence until the "consummatum est". On April 8 1934, Low Sunday, she took her perpetual vows.

In the convent she undertook the work of cook, doorkeeper and cobbler. Her ordinary life will always pass in daily penitence and self-denial in the fulfillment of the tasks assigned to her. The exceptional nature of her adventure, however, totally unfolded in the intimacy of her spirit. True contemplative, the whole world and every creature in need of compassion was shared between God and her. Through grace, rather with the love that joins than with the sensibility of the mystical gift, she became the confidante of the Sacred Heart that is perfectly human, as the Lord himself taught her : *"Do not make me a harsh God while I am no less than the God of love!"*.

Through Consolata God seemed to want to educate the heart of man anew to the union with Him; between creature and Creator no longer servile subordination, rather intimacy. This is, in substance, the spiritual content of the supplication "Jesus, Mary I love you, save souls," the characteristic of the Tiny Path of Love shown by the Lord to the humble Capuchin nun to bring back to grace and compassion, with a simple act of confidence, millions of souls tormented by sin. Was especially merit of Father Lorenzo Sales (1889-1972), her confessor and spiritual director from September 1935, to have helped with wisdom and discernment the Work of God written more in the life of Sister Consolata than in the notes of her diary. In this Work of charity she was firstly subjected to every trial that requires in man pure faith in Him, who can do all. Consolata will come to moan: *"I feel all the passions of capital sins are rioting in me"*. But the Divine Bridegroom, in this martyrdom *"until the last drop of blood"* to save the world, also assured her: *"Since I am the Most Holy it is my thirst to communicate it to souls ... You only love. You are too small to climb to the summit: I will carry you on my shoulders".*

3. MARTYRDOM OF LOVE

In November 1944 she notes: *"For many days my soul has halted on this divine phrase - 'Sacrificial victim for sacrificial victim'".* It is in this way that, for the peace of the world, for the dying and for all souls she many times repeats the offer of herself as the sacrifice of expiation, as true contemplative who intercedes for the whole humanity. In particular, that redeeming love which rendered her crucified with the Crucifix was for those who, also called to it in the special way of following Christ, lacked faithfulness because overcome by sin.

On November 9 1934 Consolata wrote: *"Jesus revealed to me the intimate sufferings of His Heart caused by the faithlessness of souls consecrated to Him".* We thus enter into the deepest throbbing of her interior world, that which would bring her with generosity to the *"summit of pain"* and to a boundless maternity of souls to bring to salvation. Jesus and Consolata: together in love, together in pain, together to deliver back millions of souls to the Father rich in Compassion.

On September 24 1945 Sister Consolata asked for half a day of rest and she laid down. The Mother Abbess took her temperature - nearly 39°! How long has she been carrying on like this? In June

1939 she let drop a phrase from her pen: *"It costs me to die in little pieces"*.

To her hidden condition of illness and to her stern life of penitence will be added in short, as well, the hardships of the years of the Second World War. Consolata will literally suffer from hunger, but with the generosity of always: she will transform this tragedy into *"an ascetic theology of the appetite"*! It is the last act of love: the one that will cost her her life. In winter 1944 her corpse-like color betrays her. In obedience she subjects herself to a medical visit. The doctor's reply was *"simply"* : *"This sister is not ill, she is destroyed"*. On October 25 1945 the X-ray reveals the damage to her lungs. On November 4 she leaves for the sanatorium. She will remain there until July 3 1946, when an ambulance will return her, in the last stages of consumption, to the Convent of Moriondo. Now, *"everything is finished"*, to begin again in Heaven. The Sister dies at dawn on July 18. The *"regal Te Deum"* of her life is fulfilled in the transfiguration of a single prayer: *"I love you, Lord, my strength!"* (Ps 17, 2).

4. THE TOPICALITY OF A MESSAGE

Sister Maria Consolata Betrone was a mystic favored by locutions and, perhaps, by visions of Jesus. She reported it precisely in her diary, carefully examined by Father Lorenzo Sales, Consolata Missionary, at first skeptical and unsure, then in his turn divulger of the Work of the Lord.
"Humble and great, active and contemplative, serene and tormented, suffering and full of joy, Consolata led a linear life reconciling each differing thing in herself and unifying everything in the ardent love of God.

Long and intensely tempted herself, she had a delicate understanding of sinners, especially for consecrated souls who had transgressed, and for their conversion she offered God all her suffering and pain and finished by offering life itself". This Poor Clare nun was presented in these words in the statement which introduced the beatification process. Here is revealed a spirituality of atonement perfectly in harmony with that desire for penitence which inspired the beginnings of her vocation. A mystic is always inserted in the context of his or her historical times and by it is inspired and *"sent"* by God. She is a sort of *"prophet"* open to the spiritual needs of her contemporary humanity and in the same way offers herself with Christ to the Father.

In the heart of a century dedicated to sin, to atheism and, finally, religious indifference, the message of life and prayer of Sister Consolata Betrone stands out with obvious clarity as reparation and antidote to the culture of spiritual death of man. The Tiny Path of Love given in the prayer: "Jesus, Mary, I love you, save souls," is not only a brief prayer, rather an interior way able to educate and promote a greater confidence between man and his God in the knowledge and faith full of that great divine attribute that is Compassion. Through this very simple way, the soul is newly returned to vital communion with the Most High in the true capacity of its own contemplative dimension. Consolata Betrone was not alone in this tracing of the return route of the *"prodigal son"*, XX century man, to a Father rich in Compassion. The broad Divine plan seem to have significantly interwoven her human and mystic existence with those of two of her *"distant"* contemporaries: Sister Maria Faustina Kowalska (1905-1938) and the monk Silvanus of Mount Athos (1866-1938). The common denominator of all is Thérèse of Lisieux (1837-1897).

In the culture of making and having, re-proposing the evangelical need *"to pray continually and never lose heart"* (Lk 18,1), the message sent to us by Sister Consolata assumes the importance of a gospel for our time. A gospel of love, of hope and compassion for the years of hate, desperation and distance from God. God offers the remedy of spiritual breath to man suffocated by materialism. A contemporary *"Clare"* again announces the need for the primacy of God in the heart of man.

x

CHILDREN OF MARY

Children of Mary is a semi-contemplative Community of Sisters founded in 2002 whose charism is to quench the Thirst of Jesus to be loved in the Most Blessed Sacrament. They do this with their own love: attending daily Mass and receiving Jesus in Holy Communion, daily adoration, and a life of prayer, work and ministry, spreading the great news of Jesus Eucharistic and encouraging others to return love for Love. Their ministries include parish missions, retreat work, leading Holy Hours, teaching and praying at schools, soup kitchens, prisons, nursing homes and the dying, wherever they are invited! They also make and distribute prayer cards, CDs, DVDs and books.

Children of Mary Motherhouse is located in the Archdiocese of Cincinnati. They also have a retreat house in the Columbus Diocese located in Newark, OH. For more information about the Sisters or their apostolates, please visit: www.childrenofmary.net.

81720646R00150

Made in the USA
Columbia, SC
07 December 2017